MW00986499

SPIRITUAL DIRECTION 101

THE BASICS OF SPIRITUAL GUIDANCE

TERESA BLYTHE

Apocryphile Press

1700 Shattuck Ave #81, Berkeley, CA 94709

www.apocryphilepress.com

Copyright © 2018 by Teresa Blythe

Printed in the United States of America

ISBN 978-1-947826-20-5

All rights reserved. No part of this book may be reproduced, stored in a retrieval system, or transmitted in any form or by any means—electronic, mechanical, photocopy, recording, or otherwise—without written permission of the author and publisher, except for brief quotations in printed reviews. Printed in the United States of America

Teresa Blythe photo by Duane Schneider

Please join our mailing list at
www.apocryphilepress.com/free
We'll keep you up-to-date on all our new releases,
and we'll also send you a FREE BOOK.
Visit us today!

This book is dedicated to the administrators, faculty and graduates of the Hesychia School of Spiritual Direction at the Redemptorist Renewal Center in Tucson, Arizona.

CONTENTS

INTRODUCTION

Nothing is as deep or as personal as one's feelings about God. Finding someone who has the experience and skill to help you explore the realm of the Divine is like finding water in the desert.

So where is an experienced and confident spiritual director when you need one? As the number of people seeking spiritual guidance grows, that becomes a crucial question.

Each year dozens of spiritual direction training programs graduate people with certificates of completion. So why is it sometimes hard to find a spiritual director who welcomes new directees? I believe it is that many people trained in the art of spiritual direction need a greater sense of how to conduct a meaningful spiritual direction session in order to confidently invite people into direction.

It's time to bridge a gap that exists in the world of spiritual direction.

Most training programs share a core belief in how spiritual direction is done. However, they also have different requirements and areas of emphasis. At present, there is no agreed-upon curriculum or set of standards a training program must meet in order to operate. That is not necessarily a bad thing—there are good reasons for not requiring standard certification of programs or spiritual directors. We're dealing with matters of the spirit and people from a variety of religious traditions so it would be hard (some say impossible) to come up with standards that everyone agrees upon.

The spiritual direction training program I graduated from, the Diploma in the Art of Spiritual Direction from San Francisco Theological Seminary, took over two years to complete and included history, theory, theology, spiritual formation and what seemed like an excessive amount of practicum—classes where you must do spiritual direction in front of a teacher and classmates. When I left SFTS and moved to Arizona, I was shocked to encounter spiritual directors saying, "I have a certificate from XYZ program, but I can't say I know how to sit for an hour with someone in spiritual direction." When I would ask why, it was always because the program didn't spend much time on practical skills.

Part of the reason for this is a basic philosophical difference found within the spiritual direction community worldwide centering around the question: Is spiritual direction a charism (gift from God) that need only be developed in the gifted person, or is it something that can be taught widely? The programs that fall into the "mostly a gift" category exist primarily to develop the gift in people they determine to be gifted. These programs rely heavily on the screening of their applicants. Other programs hedge a bit and say that if a person is properly formed through training, then they may discern if they are gifted to be a spiritual director, and if so, be taught. In either case, practical skills may be secondary.

I consider practical skills primary.

No matter how you understand a calling to spiritual direction, and no matter how you choose to be in spiritual formation, you can learn the basic practical skills of spiritual direction! You may or may not later want to hang out a shingle and call yourself a spiritual director. But you can learn the basics, which will (I can almost guarantee) form you into a better and more deeply spiritual person with a greater capacity for compassion for yourself and others.

And so, I have created this primer to share the basics of spiritual guidance. It won't cover everything you need to know, and at times it will repeat important information that applies to more than one chapter. Spiritual Direction 101 focuses less on how you are spiritually formed as a director—there are a host of excellent books on that topic—and more on what to do when you are meeting with someone, whether formally or informally, who needs spiritual guidance.

The content for this book is from the program I direct, the Hesychia School of Spiritual Direction at the Redemptorist Renewal Center in Tucson, Arizona. At Hesychia, our top goal is proficiency. We don't want anyone leaving our program saying they don't know how to do spiritual direction!

A Word about Language and Terminology

One of the challenges of creating a practical guide is to use language that is straightforward, inclusive and understandable to all who read it. Wherever possible, I prefer common terminology over spiritual jargon, and I seek to write so that people from a variety of faith traditions and backgrounds feel welcomed and supported.

I am writing about a practice that goes by different names. My preferred term for our subject is spiritual direction, since that is the term that seems to be most recognizable (to those who give and receive spiritual guidance). I will also at times use the term spiritual guide or spiritual companion. Some spiritual guides refer to the people they work with as directees; others use the term clients or companions.

Some people are comfortable talking about God and others find God-language off-putting. I don't want any of my words to be a stumbling block. So throughout the book, so I will vary the terms commonly used for the Divine, and humbly ask the reader to bear with me when I use a term that is not a fit for you.

WHAT YOU WILL FIND IN THIS BOOK

PART ONE explains what contemporary spiritual direction is (Chapter 1) and then explains some of the history (Chapter 2), and theological underpinnings of the practice (Chapter 3).

PART TWO is the heart of the book. Chapter 4 illustrates and explains in everyday terms the most popular, safe and effective method used today in spiritual direction, known as the evocative or non-directive method. Chapter 5 shares the tools directors use to attend and respond to content directees bring and provides a list of helpful questions a director may ask in a session. And Chapter 6 describes the many forms of spiritual direction, including individual, couples, group and organizational direction.

Spiritual direction in today's world must include an understanding of how to work across gender, culture and faith traditions. Chapter 7 offers general guidelines for working with someone whose life experience and background is quite different from your own. Because the evocative method is open-ended and non-sectarian, it lends itself to a multi-faith practice.

Also included in this section is a chapter (8) on how spiritual direction differs from a lot of other helping professions, including psychological counseling, pastoral counseling, prayer partnering, life coaching and more.

PART THREE centers on the ethical considerations essential to the practice of spiritual guidance and how to become a spiritual director. Chapter 9 covers important ethical issues, including: boundary awareness and setting; transference and countertransference; the handling of dual or multiple relationships with directees; how to begin and end spiritual direction relationships; and mandated reporting of child and elder abuse.

Since most spiritual directors today need to demonstrate that they have received a certificate of completion in a training program, Chapter 10 is designed to help the prospective spiritual director discern what kind of formation and training program is right for them.

Chapter 11 provides basic business advice about the work as a spiritual director—setting up a practice and telling the world about it. This chapter can help a newly trained spiritual guide figure out what sort of practice they are suited for; how much to charge in fees; what kind of physical space they need in order to meet with people; and appropriate ways to use technology in their practice.

In addition to these four sections, you will find at the end of the book a list of *Works Cited* and a *Topical Reading List* about issues related to spiritual guidance and spirituality in general.

DIVE RIGHT IN

It is my hope that this book will "get your feet wet" and inspire you to dive in and study more about spiritual direction. Or perhaps it will get a conversation started about what spiritual guidance means for you.

If you are thinking of becoming a spiritual director, I hope this book helps your decision-making process. If you already are a practicing spiritual director, I hope what I have written helps you feel more confident in your work.

I welcome questions, comments, observations and reflections from you about what you read here. I may be reached at teresa@teresablythe.net.

May your path be blessed.

WHAT IS SPIRITUAL DIRECTION?

Jeff walks into his spiritual director's office wracked with emotional pain over news reports about a religious leader claiming the world was coming to an end that week. He wants to believe in a God of unconditional love—which is what his faith community teaches—but he can't seem to overcome the fear left over from spending his formative years in an "our way or the highway" church. The spiritual director maintains a calm, loving presence as she listens to Jeff. She doesn't seem alarmed or try to talk him out of his fear, which is so different from the way his friends react if and when he dares to open up to them. They just laugh at him and say, "How could anyone be afraid of such predictions?"

But the spiritual director responds kindly. She asks him about the God he believes in. She listens as he describes two images of God: the one he could love; and the one he grew up with—the one he is afraid of.

As he describes the God he wants to trust, the spiritual director encourages him to reflect on times in his life when he may have encountered that God—perhaps even unknowingly. They take a long period of silence and suddenly he remembers a moment of all-encompassing love and freedom that came over him one day when he was walking on campus at his college. He felt a presence that seemed to say, "You have no need to fear me anymore."

From the moment he recalled that experience of the Divine, Jeff began to develop a relationship with *that* presence, using that mystical moment in his life as a benchmark.

That's spiritual direction.

That's what can happen when a spiritual guide creates a safe space for someone to be vulnerable. It's the wonder of helping someone discover the difference between the God of their experience and the God someone else told them to believe in.

DEFINITIONS

You've picked up this book because you want to know more about the art and ministry called spiritual direction (spiritual guidance or spiritual companioning), an ancient practice experiencing a revival in our culture. There are, as you may imagine, many definitions of spiritual direction—all rich in description.

Here's one to start with:

> *Spiritual direction is the exploration of a person's spiritual path with someone trained in listening, deep reflection and discernment.*

Those are all carefully chosen, important words. So let's break it down.

Spiritual direction is an exploration. It's a gentle, open-ended conversation between a spiritual guide and a client (frequently called directee or companion). When we explore, we take time to ponder, question, reflect and consider a spiritual path. Exploration implies freedom and it is essential that directees feel free and unfettered in what they share with a spiritual guide.

The path being explored belongs solely to the directee. For the person seeking spiritual direction, the time spent with a spiritual director is about taking the next step along their spiritual path—not taking a step someone else thinks they ought to take. This is a most important distinction.

The path is spiritual. Directors are not therapists poking around a person's psyche. Spiritual guides understand that all of life is spiritual—the Spirit is found in all our experiences. With that understanding, spiritual directors will explore with clients many aspects of life. But we keep the emphasis on spirituality.

Spiritual directors are trained to listen. In our culture today, listening is a lost art. The kind of intent, deep and holy listening that spiritual guides do requires training.

We are trained in deep reflection. Spiritual guides learn how to interact with clients so that they may reflect more deeply into areas of life where they find the most meaning.

Spiritual directors are trained in the principles of discernment— wisdom and processes for making choices in alignment with the person's highest values and understanding of the Divine.

Other definitions of spiritual direction include:

"Helping people deepen their intimacy with the Divine." –Rev. John Mabry, Director of the Chaplaincy Institute's Interfaith Spiritual Direction Certificate Program in Berkeley

"Spiritual direction is the practice of being attentive to God's life and movement in our human quest for meaning, love and our true identity." —*Hesychia School of Spiritual Direction at the Redemptorist Renewal Center in Tucson*

"Spiritual direction explores a deeper relationship with the spiritual aspect of being human. Simply put, spiritual direction is helping people tell their sacred stories every day." —Spiritual Directors International's definition on its "What is Spiritual Direction?" webpage.[1]

Pick up any book on spiritual direction and you will find different definitions. If you are a spiritual guide or are considering training to become one, you will need to develop your own definition. If you are a person seeking spiritual direction, ask prospective guides how they define the practice of spiritual guidance. Their answer will help you decide if they are a good fit for you.

It's helpful to use metaphors to describe the role of the spiritual director.

Spiritual Director as Field Guide

Spiritual directors today are like field guides along the spiritual walk, pointing out interesting highlights and asking directees to think more deeply about certain questions. As a field guide, it is hoped that we will at least recognize the terrain.

A field guide observes the walk with the person we are guiding, aware that God is leading the way and is in relationship with them the whole time. The field guide knows the spiritual path somewhat because the guide has walked his or her own path, and has walked alongside others. At the same time, the field guide knows that no two walks are ever the same and approaches each experience with humility and wonder.

One way we are different from the field guide leading a nature tour is that they usually do a lot of talking about the path. Spiritual directors, however, are more silent. We're more likely to ask questions about what the directees see, hear, feel and experience. Our job is to direct attention to places along the path that might be worth exploring more carefully and deeply.

Spiritual Director as Accompanist

Similarly, spiritual directors are like backup musicians, playing the accompaniment for a soloist who has a beautiful song to sing.

If you think of the directee as the soloist, and the song as the story of their spiritual life, the director is given the duty to stay right with the song. We don't run ahead of the soloist or lag behind. Just like the accompanist, we listen carefully and do our best to only play notes that enhance the song.

Spiritual Director as Couples Counselor

Rev. John Mabry, director of the Chaplaincy Institute's Interfaith Spiritual Direction Certificate Program in Berkeley, CA, uses the metaphor of couples counselor, with the couple being the directee and the Divine, "helping this couple achieve the intimacy that they both, in their heart of hearts, desperately desire."[2] This image fits well with Spiritual Directors International's description of the practice of honoring the "third chair."[3] By third chair, they mean the acknowledgment of a third person in all spiritual guidance conversations—the Holy One. Remembering the presence of this third chair helps spiritual directors and clients stay focused on what really matters.

WHO SEEKS SPIRITUAL DIRECTION?

There is no one type of person looking for spiritual direction. Certainly, many Christian clergy and religious professionals have sought it. But over the last 50 years, the practice has blossomed so that seekers (and practitioners) of spiritual direction come from all walks of life.

Seekers come from all socio-economic classes. They are male and female. Young and old. Married and single. Lesbian, gay, bisexual, transgender and straight. Some directees are very religious, while others fall into the "spiritual but not religious" category. They are agnostics and lifelong believers. Many are from 12-step or other recovery programs. They come from a variety of religious traditions. Although spiritual direction as discussed in this book grew out of the contemplative side of Christianity (primarily the Catholic branch), not all people who visit spiritual directors are Christian, nor is there any expectation they would become one as a result of being in spiritual direction. You now find spiritual directors and directees who are Jewish, Hindu, Sufi-Muslim, Buddhist, interfaith and interspiritual.

Many names for God are used in spiritual direction—Higher Power, Spirit, Creator, Unseen Reality, Source of Life, the Divine, Goddess, Sophia, Wisdom, Divine Light, Holy One (the list goes on and on).

What we can safely say about people who come to spiritual direction is that they are seeking greater awareness of the sacred in their life. Some are people wondering "where is God in this situation I am facing?" Some find their spiritual connection to the Source of Life is growing and they want to savor and celebrate that. Others feel their relationship to the Holy is stale and they want to understand and remedy that. Some have had a profound or even disturbing religious experience and need help processing what it means for them.

Many come to spiritual direction because they need to make a crucial decision and want help in discerning a path forward. Groups or organizations may request spiritual direction because they want to be more attentive to the Spirit, but aren't sure exactly what that means for them. Countless people seek spiritual direction because they have lost sight of God's desire for them in the "busy-ness" of life, and they believe a spiritual director would help them see more clearly again. And others want a spiritual director simply because they crave time with someone who will listen to them and support them as they talk about things that really matter—prayer, the meaning of life, their values and ethical choices.

Much like the poem about people coming into our life for "a reason, a season or a lifetime,"[4] people come to spiritual direction for different reasons and lengths of time. Since the practice is so centered on the seeker, how they use spiritual direction is entirely up to them.

THE MOST POPULAR METHOD

Almost all spiritual direction formation and training programs teach a non-directive, or what we will call in this book, an evocative method of guidance. Chapter 4 will go into this method extensively. In brief, it is a style of accompaniment that combines deep listening, open-ended questions, an invitation to reflection and awareness, and assistance with discernment.

WHAT SPIRITUAL DIRECTION CAN DO

Spiritual direction can help a person become more aware of where the Divine is active and moving in their life. In it, we savor and remember God's goodness and discern how it is we are being invited to reach out to others in a broken and hurting world. Spiritual direction is also helpful for people moving through tough spiritual questions that arise when one's image of God is malformed or arrested in time, or when recovering from past religious or spiritual abuse. Questions about a powerful religious experience are welcomed and nurtured in spiritual direction.

As mentioned earlier, one of the most helpful aspects of spiritual direction is assistance with the spiritual practice of discernment. In Pierre Wolff's classic book on discernment in the Ignatian tradition, *Discernment: The Art of Choosing Well*, he writes:

> *Discernment is the process of making choices that correspond as closely*
> *as possible to objective reality, that are as free as possible from our inner*
> *compulsions, and that are closely attuned to the convictions of our faith*
> *(or to our value system, if we have no religious belief).*[5]

Discernment involves listening—in prayer and reflection—to

insight from our Higher Power, our intellect, and our bodies about a choice we are facing. Listening in silence for clarity around a question is a key component of discernment, and is the primary way people in the Quaker tradition make serious choices. Spiritual directors, especially those trained in discernment processes, make excellent sounding boards for people facing important crossroads in life.

Finally, spiritual direction can be a wonderful complement to psychological counseling. Although some psychologists are attuned to the spiritual aspects of life, most are not trained as spiritual directors. Some patients in counseling find they want to take certain insights from counseling into spiritual direction for exploration. This works well as long as it is understood that spiritual direction is a complement to therapy, not a replacement for it.

WHAT SPIRITUAL DIRECTION CANNOT DO

Spiritual direction is not professional counseling, even though there are overlapping practices, such as active listening. Spiritual direction is a wellness practice, not a problem-solving practice. First and foremost, spiritual directors do not diagnose or treat any disorder of any kind. For example, if a person is clearly suffering from depression, a good spiritual director will likely notice that and refer the person to a mental health professional. As the depression is being treated on a physical and emotional level, the depressed person may also seek spiritual direction to reflect upon how God is present to them in the midst of this situation. But a good spiritual director will not expect spiritual guidance to solve a psychological problem. (Much more will be said about these distinctions in Chapter 8.)

Spiritual guidance is not about "fixing" problems. People bring all of who they are to spiritual direction, and since life is full of problems, spiritual directors hear about problems—a lot. But we are not looking to fix anything. Problems are like storms on the sea—to be expected now and then. The spiritual director may help the person navigate their boat in the storm but cannot and will not steer the boat for the person. Spiritual directors expect that God and the individual will weather the storm together. We are there to help the individual notice how the Spirit is leading them in the midst of the situation. What is the sacred invitation in this situation?

Spiritual direction is never about telling people what to do in any given situation. A good spiritual director invites a person to look inside themselves, to their own wisdom, for those answers.

If you are considering becoming a spiritual director, you need to carefully consider what you think spiritual direction is and come up with a working definition of it for your practice. Working your way through this book will help you do that.

Some questions to ponder:

- What draws you to spiritual direction?
- What is your definition of the practice?
- If you are in spiritual direction, how does this chapter's description of spiritual direction reflect what your director does?
- If you are a spiritual director, do the metaphors used in this chapter (field guide, couples' counselor, accompanist) fit for you? How do you see yourself in relation to your clients?

NOTES

1. SDI web page found at http://www.sdiworld.org/find-a-spiritual-director/what-is-spiritual-direction
2. Personal email conversation with John Mabry April 15, 2017.

3. Description of the three chairs can be found on SDI's web page http://www.sdiworld.org/about-us/purpose-and-history/three-chairs.
4. Poem "Reason, Season or Lifetime," sometimes attributed to Eleanor Roosevelt. However, the actual author is unknown. Check it out at https://www.theodysseyonline.com/the-reason-season-or-lifetime among others.
5. Pierre Wolf. *Discernment: The Art of Choosing Well."* Liguori, MO: Liguori Publications, 1970.

2

HISTORY AND BACKGROUND OF
SPIRITUAL DIRECTION

EARLY HISTORY

Since the beginning of human history, people have sought wisdom about life beyond the material world from others who seemed to have a connection with it. In that way, spiritual guidance is prehistoric.

What we now think of as spiritual direction dates back to the 3rd century Desert Fathers and Mothers. These rugged Christians withdrew to the Egyptian desert outside of Alexandria and attempted to live the life of an ascetic—fasting, praying, singing psalms and living alone in caves or small cells.

At the time of the desert monastics, Christianity had become the national, accepted religion in Rome and many followers felt the tradition was too institutionalized and no longer had its "edge." Seekers longed for a simpler devotion, and they looked to these desert hermits for direction.

The most famous of the desert monastics, Anthony of Egypt, was born into a wealthy family but later took Jesus literally in the teaching, "If you want to be perfect, go, sell what you have and give to the poor, and you will have treasures in heaven."(Mt 19:21)

11

Anthony left for the desert and spent years pursuing holiness, battling his inner demons and living as a hermit.

Those who came to the desert seeking "salvation" asked the elders for a "word" that would help them find it—a verbum salutis, *a "word of salvation."–Thomas Merton,* The Wisdom of the Desert (12)

Later in Anthony's life, he moved into an abandoned fort and allowed pilgrims to come to the outside of the fort and speak with him through a crevice. People traveled miles to receive one small piece of spiritual guidance from Anthony. For that reason, Anthony is considered one of the earliest spiritual directors.

Desert hermitages led to groupings of ascetics in small towns in the desert. These became the first Christian monasteries. Out of this movement came many religious communities (Catholic orders) dedicated to a life of poverty, piety and spiritual teaching.

For hundreds of years, about the only people receiving what we now think of as spiritual direction were Catholic priests, nuns and monks—and usually it was from elders in their communities. Also, for Catholics, there is a centuries-long history of spiritual direction being combined with the practice of confession, which limited who was able to offer spiritual direction. For much of the history of the practice in the Christian tradition, the goal of spiritual direction was to form people (primarily priests, brothers and nuns) into more orthodox and faithful leaders.[1]

That is no longer the case for most spiritual directors. And today, spiritual guidance is found in almost every wisdom tradition on earth.

20TH CENTURY BOOM

To understand the recent history of spiritual direction, we have to consider a bit of the history of psychology in the mid-20th century. As attendance in churches boomed in the U.S. after

World War II, the field of psychology was being shaped, in part, by the work of Carl Rogers, a former theology major. He was becoming popular for his "non-directive approach" of empathetic listening, his notion of unconditional positive regard for his clients, and his emphasis on personal growth.

Rogers moved in circles that included some of the most well known mainline Christian theologians of the 1950's, so his influence on contemporary spiritual direction is not surprising. His work peaked about the same time as the writings of Paul Tillich, the famous Lutheran theologian who wrote extensively about unconditional love and acceptance from God in Christ.

Influence of Psychology

In the 60's and 70's a great deal of interest grew within the Episcopalian church around the work of Swiss psychiatrist Carl Jung and the usefulness of his therapy techniques in what some would term "the cure of the soul." Jung's Guild of Pastoral Psychology and the Institute of Religion and Medicine were influential in the life of both churches and psychotherapists. Spirituality began to be seen as part of the whole of life—incorporating theology, liturgy, psychology and prayer.

This interest in psychology and its church-related partner, pastoral counseling, bloomed in the mid-20th century and probably contributed to the rise of spiritual direction. At the same time, the CEO model of ministry was being embraced and senior pastors were becoming less and less available for one-on-one meetings with congregants. The pastoral counselor, as a specialist, became the go-to counselor for referrals from clergy. In his book *Soul Friend*, Kenneth Leech points out a major difference between pastoral counseling and spiritual direction (although he refers to the spiritual director as "priest," which is no longer accurate):

The priest is primarily concerned with spirituality as the fundamental requirement of health. The therapist or counselor is primarily concerned with sickness. They move within the same realm of reality, and so it is not surprising that there is considerable overlap. But the priest is a spiritual director, not a therapist, and spiritual direction is not the same as therapy.[7]

Interest from Protestant Christians

Prior to the 1970's, Protestant Christians may have heard of pastoral counseling, but as a whole they were not terribly interested in one-on-one spiritual direction. Some believed it could undermine the place of Christ as the one mediator between humans and God. Certainly, spiritual practices such as prayer, worship, ethical living, journaling and receiving instruction in the Christian life were important. But private consultations with a guide just didn't register with many Protestants.

The popularity of Trappist monk Thomas Merton's writings and a growing interest in meditation techniques from the Eastern religions helped propel the practice of contemplative living into what it is today. Merton wrote about spiritual direction, as did popular writer and Dutch priest Henri Nouwen. As the writings of these men made their way beyond Catholic circles, more people began to consider contemplative spirituality and entering into spiritual direction.

Catholic religious and many Episcopal priests were already in spiritual direction when the ecumenical movement of the 80's saw the cross-fertilization of theological thought and the building of relationships between Catholics, Episcopalians, Methodists and people in the Reformed Tradition (Presbyterian, Congregationalists, Lutherans). As priests and ministers began to get to know one another in ecumenical and academic circles, the subject of spiritual direction undoubtedly came up because Protestant ministers began to go to spiritual direction and, more importantly, talk about their spiritual director to laypersons. As a result, many lay people who were spending a great deal of time in their pastor's offices began seeking spiritual counsel.

Out of this interest grew a number of formation and training programs for spiritual directors. People graduating from the early ones such as the Shalem Institute for Spiritual Formation in Washington, DC or the Mercy Center Burlingame in California then launched their own programs. As more people were trained in the art of spiritual direction, knowledge of the practice grew.

Spiritual Directors International

In 1989, Spiritual Directors International (SDI)—a non-profit organization for the purpose of networking and supporting spiritual directors all over the world—was born as a result of a discernment circle of spiritual directors at Mercy Center Burlingame, California. Carol Ludwig, a graduate of Shalem Institute and a member of SDI's coordinating council, writes, "... committee members surveyed spiritual directors in their local areas for nine months in 1989 and 1990. They asked what settings spiritual direction was being done and what kinds of people were coming for direction." (*Presence* 8.1: 9) Based on the results of that survey, a conference was held in Burlingame, followed by the first annual conference of SDI in 1991.

Three years later, SDI hired a San Francisco-based Presbyterian pastor and spiritual director, Jeff Gaines, as a part-time executive director. Under Jeff's leadership, SDI created a web presence and continued to grow.

Each year, SDI would hold an international conference the week after Easter (it still does), and each year participation in the conferences grew. Keynote speakers would present on cutting-edge topics, and workshops related to spiritual direction would bring directors from all over the world together.

The leadership of SDI could not help but notice the proliferation of formation and training programs and how diverse they all were. Shalem Institute taught a blend of contemplative practices, drawing heavily from a Quaker model for spiritual direction (silence and open-ended queries), the Dominican Center for Religious Development had what it called "the religious experience" model and of course the Jesuit-based programs had their Ignatian model.

As SDI grew and become increasingly diverse a critical issue arose: *Should spiritual directors be certified?* At the request of insurance companies, the Episcopal Church came up with guidelines for directors. But then SDI began to wonder about the ramifications of allowing insurance companies to set the standards. The core leaders of SDI formed an ethics task force that created the *SDI Guidelines for Ethical Conduct* ratified in 1999 (*Presence* 8.2: 23-24).

SDI has continued to remain neutral toward efforts to establish a standard certification, not wanting to create a standard in the U.S. that spiritual directors worldwide might find oppressive. And though it strongly recommends that spiritual directors go through formation and training, SDI refuses to endorse any program.

Another reason standard certification or licensure has not been popular involves the notion of separation of church and state. In the field of psychology, state standards vary widely and can be quite restrictive. How would an organization such as SDI be able to set standards for a practice that is as diverse as spiritual direction?

Interestingly enough, an attorney and spiritual director who helped develop the SDI ethical guidelines in the late 90's, Bill Creed, wrote an essay in the book *Sacred is the Call* in 2005 that challenges SDI's stance against standard certification for spiritual directors. He writes:

Certification or licensing of spiritual directors is needed to ensure that spiritual directors receive basic formation and evaluation. Accreditation standards need to be developed for formation programs. (156)

So, the tension around certification remains.

WHERE ARE WE HEADED?

There are currently over six thousand members of SDI worldwide. As more and more lay people, seekers and "spiritual but not religious" people discover spiritual direction and pass the word along to friends, more spiritual directors will be needed. Even though there are many training programs graduating spiritual directors each year, the trend seems to be that only a handful of those graduates actually end up practicing individual spiritual direction. And of those who do, only a tiny percentage do it full time or even half time. Most spiritual directors see only three to five people a month. That being the case, the need for spiritual guidance is hardly fading away.

NOTES

1. For an in-depth treatment of the history of spiritual direction in the Christian tradition, see Chapter 2 of Kenneth Leech's classic *Soul Friend: An Invitation to Spiritual Direction.*
2. *Ibid.*, p. 101. We will consider the differences between spiritual direction and other helping professions more fully in Chapter 8.

3

THEOLOGIES AND SPIRITUAL DIRECTION

W e are all theologians. Every time we ponder the meaning of life, the role of suffering and evil in the world, or how the world came to be—we are doing theology, defined as "God-talk." If you do it without realizing it, you are working from a kind of embedded theology—one you learned or picked up as a child. If you do it intentionally, you are working from a chosen or overt theology.

Theology encompasses all religions with the possible exception of some Buddhist traditions that are non-theistic (no concept of a deity). And there are, of course, many ways of talking about the Divine.

There are some spiritual direction training programs (mostly evangelical Christian) that embrace a strict doctrine. But most do not. Why do we not usually teach doctrine; hand out moral absolutes; offer our wisdom as a way of helping fix a situation; or move a person down a particular path? It's not the job of the spiritual director. Experience has taught that allowing the client to explore his or her own path within the framework of their chosen beliefs is safe and effective for spiritual growth.

Dogma, doctrine, and questions of orthodoxy or religious

teachings are left in the hands of institutional religion. Spiritual directors many times work outside institutions or, in some cases, on the periphery.

The *Code of Ethics for Spiritual Directors* explains why we do not interfere in a directee's belief system by steering him this way or that.

Directors do not have their own agendas and expectations for directees—other than the broad goal of a closer walk with God—but seek with each person to discern God's unique and sacred plan in that person's life.

They respect others' religious convictions and never proselytize for their own religious denomination or theological or psychological points of view, even though they are willing to be appropriately open about their own commitment to these (e.g., particular forms of prayer, tithing, the Twelve Steps, etc.)[1]

Spiritual guides also take this non-intervention position because of the Golden Rule: what we do not want others to do to us (steer us around) we do not do to others.

THEOLOGICAL FOUNDATIONS IN SPIRITUAL DIRECTION

Anytime we talk about theology in spiritual direction we are speaking of *practical* theology and not a theoretical or systematic one. This chapter will touch on a few notions about ultimate reality and our relationship to it, but more importantly, it will point you to some working theologies for spiritual directors hoping to practice this ministry in a multi-faith context. The following are a few theological assumptions that are the foundation for most formation and training programs.

Theological Assumption #1:
The Divine is real and desires a union of love with us.

Whether you prefer the term "God" or some other term for the unseen reality that is the source of all life, spiritual direction holds as foundational that this creative life force exists; the force is good and desires a two-way relationship of love with us. There may be many ways to understand this relationship—and many spiritual directors and clients reject the notion of a personal God who interacts with us in a one-on-one manner. They may balk at the second half of that assumption—that God desires something from or with us. In most cases, both director and directee work with the understanding that this relationship (between Creator and creature) is a benevolent one. Spiritual directors help people open up to this union and explore what that love means for them.

Theological Assumption #2:
We are made for relationship.

This incredible Divine essence we sometimes call God lives in relationship with all of creation. God is not separate from creation but lives and breathes in all creatures, past, present, and future. Spiritual direction is the intentional, conscious invitation to experience this embodied Presence. By maintaining an empowering and non-coercive relationship with the client, the spiritual guide fosters a more aware consciousness of God and how God is leading them in their life.

Theological Assumption #3:
All we need is written in our hearts.

"It is not too high or too far away—the word is in your hearts for you to observe" (Deuteronomy 30:10-20). Spiritual directors believe the Divine is already at work in the hearts and minds of our directees, drawing them closer to love and leading them on a good path. The spiritual practice of discernment—in which people pray and seek holy guidance along their journey—is the practice of trusting that God's desire for our directees is written on *their* hearts for *them* to observe. We help them locate it, honor it and trust in it. This theological assumption is the reason the evocative method of spiritual direction places the responsibility for a directee's choices and understanding of God squarely on the directee. In addition, by our own experience of a loving God, we as spiritual guides trust that the path of Divine love is one that will increase love and peace.

Theological Assumption #4:
Spiritual connection is developed through spiritual practice.

When we are in love with a person, we stay connected to that person. The same is true with the Divine. To be in a living, loving relationship with the Source of Life, we need to cultivate that relationship through regular spiritual practice such as prayer, reflection, meditation, fasting, study, and/or worship. Spiritual directors encourage regular spiritual practice. In the evocative method, we expect the directee to choose the spiritual practice for themselves. However, at times we may suggest a practice that seems to fit the person's situation. The life of the spiritual director can be a model for others, which is why a wise guide maintains their own regular spiritual practice.

Theological Assumption #5: The Mystery we call God
is bigger than any religious or spiritual tradition.

We each come from our own religious or spiritual tradition and our directees do as well. Dogma and doctrine are ways humans within institutions have sought to understand God, and as such they have their place. Spiritual direction works in a different realm--the realm of what we *experience* of God, even while understanding that beliefs about God influence one's experience.

Theological Assumption #6:
The true director is the Spirit.

This assumption is essential to keeping spiritual directors humble. We may think we know where a person is being led but *we don't know.* If we stick to the evocative method—where we listen, observe, gently prompt and ask open-ended questions—we allow the Spirit room to do the work. We are non-directive because God is wholly capable of doing the directing! Our job is to trust this, even when we do not see or know what is going on inside the directee. Our trust is essential for our client's spiritual growth.

Theological Assumption #7:
We are called into a world in need of great healing.

Spiritual direction encourages the balance between contemplation and action. Discernment is not finished until some action is taken. The journey inward leads us to the journey outward, into this hurting and divided world. Spiritual directors encourage this flow "from heart to hands" by living it out in our own lives and by the kind of observations, reflections and questions we pose to directees.

These seven theological assumptions are far from exhaustive. It may be helpful for every spiritual director to come up with their own set of theological assumptions that guide their work.

SOME THEOLOGIES USEFUL FOR SPIRITUAL DIRECTORS

There are a few theologies with broad themes that can help us develop skills and sensibilities for spiritual direction.

Process Theology

For those who believe life is a journey and not a destination, there is process theology.

Process theology began as a philosophy promoted by Alfred North Whitehead and Charles Hartshorne in the mid-20th century. Readings on process theology can be quite dense, philosophical and scientific. But it is well worth learning the basics for spiritual direction because this theology deals with the "here and now" and promotes a God that is with us in our suffering—both immanent (inside us) and transcendent (beyond us).

In process theology, God is ever changing and growing as we change and grow. Creation is continually birthing new forms and working its way toward greater wholeness.

Other basic points:

- The Divine is always in relationship with creation working within all good things for a better world.
- Process theology is panentheistic. "God is in all and all is in God." This would be in opposition to other understandings of the Creator's relationship with the world. Such as:

1. Deism—A Creator who stands back and watches. The idea of a God who watches from a distance is a deistic philosophy. Many non-evangelical Christians are functional deists, feeling God does not act in the world anymore—at least not in the ways recorded in scripture.
2. Theism—An unchanging God, external to the world (yet active in the world), who miraculously shows up and acts in specific moments in history. Many Christians, especially conservative ones, are theistic.
3. Pantheism—The Divine and the world are one, indistinguishable from one another. Many nature-based

spiritualties, especially among indigenous peoples, embrace this view. Pantheism is frequently demonized by theists and dismissed by deists—so much so that to talk about pan*e*ntheism can be difficult because people confuse it with pantheism.

- God and creation are constantly in the process of becoming.
- God works through *persuasive power*. Process theology talks about the power of the Creator being power in and through, not power over.
- God creates *with* the world, not independently of it.
- Freedom pervades all of existence. Process theologian Catherine Keller in *On the Mystery* writes, "The divine is within each of us, as an influence, an influx of desire—whether or not we share that desire as our own." (123)
- Evolution is creative transformation. Process theology embraces new discoveries in science.
- The Divine feels everything that happens in just the way that it happens—feels with victims and violators.
- The Creator works faithfully throughout the universe toward the good. This means that God is fully involved in all religions and wisdom traditions of the world, calling them toward faithful community together.

It is important to emphasize that process theology rejects images of the Divine as an all-powerful controlling force or "genie-in-the-sky." Critiques of process theology usually center around the argument that "your God is too weak," and the appropriate response from a process theologian would likely be "it all depends on how you define power."

To read more about process theology, consult the writings of John B. Cobb, Marjorie Hewitt Suchocki, Catherine Keller, Bruce

Epperly and Rabbi Harold Kushner. (See the *Topical Reading List* at the end of the book for more information.)

Liberation Theologies

One would hope that spiritual guidance would result in liberation for all who seek it. Because liberation is so important to the spiritual life, a theology developed in the late 1960's by South American Catholic theologians is useful.

These priests and theologians, dismayed by the disparity between rich and poor in the countries where they worked and concerned with the kind of top-down development imposed on working class people, gathered at a conference in Medellin, Columbia in 1968 and began to write about a "theology from the underside." Influenced by Karl Marx's sociological analysis (not his religious or materialist writings), these priests promoted the biblical notion of a *preferential option for the poor*. Liberation theology has greatly influenced Black, Feminist, Womanist and Queer theologies. While this theology is intricately tied to Christian communities, it can be useful for spiritual guides from a number of traditions.

The following concepts are basic to liberation theology:

- God lives in solidarity with the poor. The faith community's primary duty in a situation of oppression is to support the oppressed.
- Liberation is tied to community and is essential to wholeness. Individual spiritual healing can only come through social transformation. We are either "saved" together or we are "lost" together.
- The story of the Exodus is the biblical paradigm. Just as the Israelites moved from slavery in Egypt to freedom in the desert and later to the promised land, people

today enslaved in poverty and oppression cry out to be moved to freedom.

- Orthodoxy (right belief) only stems from Orthopraxis (right action).
- Oppression can come in many forms: Sexism, racism, heterosexism, patriarchal religious teachings, religious abuse, domestic violence and a wide range of ways people are marginalized.
- Structures and systems that are coercive do violence to people even if no actual physical force is used.
- Openness to truth that has not yet dawned upon us is part of an authentic spiritual path.

While it may seem that liberation theology would be critical of such individualized attention as one-on-one direction might give, we find in liberation theology *themes* that help us as directors.

- God desires freedom and justice for all, especially for those who have been victimized.
- We experience the Divine in community.
- The Spirit urges us toward liberation from oppressive forces.
- Oppressors are just as broken as those they hold down. Liberation frees everyone.

To read more about liberation theology, see the writings of Jon Sobrino, Daniel L. Migliore, Gustavo Gutierrez, Leonardo Boff, and Juan Luis Segundo.

For a feminist take on liberation theology, see Mary Daly, Rosemary Radford Ruether, Judith Plaskow, Elizabeth Schussler Fiorenza, Carol Christ and Miriam Starhawk.

On black liberation theology, read James Cone, Cornel West and Dr. Martin Luther King, Jr.

Womanist theology is liberation theology from a black

woman's perspective. For more on this, read Renita Weems, Dolores Williams and Stephanie Mitchem.

Queer theology is liberation theology from a gender and sexual minority lens. Check out writers John J. McNeill, Susannah Cornwall and Patrick Cheng.

Resources from these writers are included in the *Topical Reading List*.

Incarnational Theologies

In theological circles, there is no discreet category called Incarnational Theology. However, there are some principles that could be called by this name, and they are useful for spiritual direction.

Incarnation generally refers to the Divine living and working in us. Incarnational theologies see humans as part of the great web of life created by God and co-creating with God for a brighter future.

For many Christians, incarnation refers specifically to God becoming flesh in Jesus. You find this incarnational theology in Celtic, Jesuit, Carmelite, Franciscan and Benedictine spiritualities. In the Orthodox tradition, there is the notion of *theotokos*, or God-bearer. This refers to Mary as the one who bore Jesus, but it also takes on a broader meaning for us. We are to give birth to the Spirit in the world.

Spiritual direction focuses on a relationship between the person and the Divine. We do this because of who God is—a relational being or force. In Trinitarian theology, God is three persons *in relationship*. In Unitarian theology, God is One, encompassing all that is and urging us to be in right relationship with God, humanity and creation. For non-theist traditions or for people who are spiritual but not religious, incarnation can be understood as our inner light and wisdom.

Some themes in incarnational theologies:

- We are part of the Divine and the Divine is in us, but we are not all of who God is.
- We are the face and hands of God in this world.
- The gifts of the Spirit are incarnate in us.
- Spirituality is a dynamic "dancing relationship" in which we participate with the Divine in the dance.
- Relationship with the one who gave us life is paramount.
- Creation is also incarnation. We are part of creation and have a special role to play in taking care of creation. We are stewards, not rulers of creation.

In spiritual direction, we can look for glimpses of incarnation:

- Within the directee's mind, body and spirit.
- In the directee's interpersonal relationships.
- In their relationship with nature.
- Within systems and structures of the directee's life. Systems and structures are those groups or entities that include us but have life beyond us. These entities have rules—spoken or unspoken—and histories. Families, governments, organizations, corporations, religious communities and clubs are examples of a system.

We honor the incarnation of the Divine in each directee and look for that Divine wisdom to surface in their daily lives, thoughts, feelings and insights. In spiritual direction, we enter the dance of the Spirit with them, looking for touch points of deep connection in the relationship.

To read more about theologies of incarnation, see works by Jürgen Moltmann, Graham Cole and Thomas Torrance.

NOTES

1. Hedberg and Caprio, *A Code of Ethics for Spiritual Directors*, p. 10. A longer discussion of this booklet can be found in Chapter 9 on Ethical Considerations in Spiritual Direction.

4

THE EVOCATIVE METHOD OF
SPIRITUAL DIRECTION

Many people today claim to be spiritual guides. Some are trained and others are self-appointed. It is usually best to find a spiritual director, guide or companion who has been trained in a method of guidance that is safe, effective and ethical.

Of the hundreds of programs that train spiritual directors, the majority use a method we are referring to as evocative or nondirective. This method leaves the power for change and decision in the hands of the directee. It's always about the spiritual path of the directee—not about a path the director wants a directee to take. Any spiritual director who becomes controlling and insistent on pushing a particular dogma or worldview is attempting to take personal power away from the directee. Spiritual directors are not evangelists, advocates or advisors. Instead, we watch and listen, looking for ways to help the directee find his or her way from the desires and stirrings of his or her own heart.

Basic elements of the evocative method are:

AWARENESS AND CONTEMPLATION

The first step in any spiritual journey is awareness—becoming open to a reality beyond self.

Many people enter spiritual direction to become more aware of God's presence in their life and in the world. They want their belief in a Higher Power to make that journey from head to heart. They want to *feel* the love of God so they can live in harmony with it.

Even if you seek spiritual direction for some other reason, a good director will draw your attention to awareness. You will likely be asked, "When are you most aware of God's love in your life?" Or, "How have you experienced your Higher Power lately?"

You may enter spiritual direction because you are not at all sure if you are aware of God's presence. And in spiritual direction, it's OK to admit you aren't sure "what's what!" Exploration and discovering for yourself how God interacts with you is our only goal.

Jesus spoke frequently of staying "awake and aware." So, how do we do that?

Awareness of God is enhanced primarily through:

- Dedication to a regular spiritual practice that fits your personality.
- Spending time in silence, meditation or centering prayer.
- Noticing daily where you experience life, energy, joy, peace, wisdom and other "fruits of the Spirit" that point us to God. (A daily practice of journaling about your discoveries can help).
- Talking about those experiences in life that transcend "business as usual" and seem to shimmer with holiness.

Once aware, we are invited into contemplation—a form of

quiet resting in God's embrace with no need for words or particular actions. It is what the Psalmist meant when writing, "Be still
and know I am God." The late Walter J. Burghardt, Jesuit theologian and spiritual writer, defined contemplation as "a long, loving
look at the real."[1] Once you get to what is real in your life, then
you are at a place where God is actively inviting you to a closer
relationship through awareness, prayer, discernment and action.

Most of us are drawn to one facet of the spiritual life. If you
are an introvert, you may prefer stillness and silent prayer. Extroverts may prefer more active ways of connecting with God—
spoken prayers, walking a labyrinth or chanting. The reality is, we
need all of the above.

Spiritual direction helps us take that "long, loving look at the
real" from angles we may have been neglecting. In fact, the stillness angle is probably the most neglected today. Unless we are
really careful, our lives tend toward the hectic. Our culture is so
bombarded with persuasive messages about how to live "the good
life" that we can easily lose sight of what is real and lasting.

Spiritual directors exist to remind us to connect with our
inner stillness and wait for the gentle prompting or insight from
God. Spiritual direction is a contemplative practice that helps us
recover that all-important quest for meaning, love and our true
identity.

A key component of resting in the Divine is cultivating silence.

Silence is sometimes referred to as God's first language.
Redemptorist retreat leader, Fr. Tom Santa, calls silence "the
essential nutrient of the soul."[11] But how you feel about silence
probably has a lot to do with your personality type, your neuro-
logical make-up and your upbringing. Introverts may be more
comfortable with silence than extroverts. People who were
punished with "the silent treatment" may avoid silence at all costs.

No matter how you feel about quieting down and being in
silence, I'm going to encourage you to befriend it. Even if you can
only be in silence for a few minutes a day, give it a try. Our lives

have become so loud, hurried and chaotic that our souls are starved for some downtime.

Spiritual direction reveres silence.[12] It is a place where you can begin and end a conversation with silence. We give you time to pause and be with your thoughts and feelings.

It is wise for the spiritual director to occasionally invite a period of silence and then ask, "What happened for you in the silence?" So many times, directees find a word, phrase, image or feeling that provides some clarity.

Here is a simple practice to cultivate silence:

1. Ask for the grace to be present to the Divine in the silence.
2. Let go of expectations and relax.
3. Sit for 3-5 minutes (use a timer on your cellphone if you want) in silence. Pay attention to *one* of your senses—hearing, sight, touch, taste or smell. If and when your mind wanders from that sense and jumps about, say to yourself, "I'm returning to this moment." And return to your direct experience of the present moment.
4. When time is up, say a prayer of gratitude for the sacredness of direct experience.
5. As you become more comfortable with a few minutes of silent, direct experience, expand to 10-15 minutes.

REFLECTION

Many people come to spiritual direction wanting to better understand an experience of God from their past. Perhaps it was something that happened in prayer or worship. Or it might have been an experience in daily life that opened them to a deeper sense of being loved by God. A spiritual director is trained to help the client recall times when they felt close to God or felt at one with the universe. If we stay with the memory and allow the Divine to reveal something new as a result of it, we may experience the blessing again or in a new way and we learn something new about ourselves or about God. Sitting with that memory—in silence and gratitude—helps us savor the fullness of God. Just like turning up the volume on a song you love, sitting with a past experience can amplify the experience. As you re-experience it in your imagination and senses, you change and grow.

You can do this on your own in prayer by asking the Spirit to help you remember significant moments in your life. See, hear, feel and taste those moments again in your mind and body. You may want to journal about the experience, both past and present, and also where the experience may be leading you. Lots of directees bring their journals of memories into direction for just this kind of work.

The experience you return to in prayer doesn't have to be a warm and fuzzy one. Sometimes we need to face the fearful and anxious experiences again in a safe place with a spiritual director. Until we work through them adequately, they can easily crop up as triggers that torment us. I find that spiritual direction is the perfect safe place for me to remember and face those rocky places.

One of the best tools for reflection is a practice known as the Ignatian Examen. It can be done in a number of ways, but here's a simple way to use it:

1. Become present to yourself and open yourself to a greater reality.
2. Look back at a particular time in your life (last week, last month, a particular year, etc.). Allow your mind to go over that time almost as if you were watching a video.
3. Find a moment in that period of time in which you felt most alive. What were you doing? Who were you with? Where were you? Allow yourself to re-enter that

moment and feel that life in you again. Open yourself to whatever insight this memory has to offer.

4. Find a moment in that period of time in which you felt least alive. What were you doing? Who were you with? Where were you? Allow yourself to re-enter that moment and feel that lack of life in you again. Open yourself to whatever insight this memory has to offer.

5. Sink into a deeper silence and allow the Holy to offer you an invitation, support or greater understanding as a result of revisiting this time in your life.

6. End with a prayer of gratitude.

DISCERNMENT

The spiritual practice of discernment grows out of our awareness and trust in the Divine. Discernment asks the question, "What is the Divine inviting me to be or do in this situation?" Whenever we come to an important choice in life—what work to pursue, who to be in relationship with, how to spend our time, effort and money—we may want to know what God wants for us. Spiritual directors, especially those trained in discernment, can help a person sort through the facts, practical considerations, gut feelings and insights in order to come to some clarity about the choice.

Discernment is less about a process (although there are many processes you can use) than about a way of life. Our one and only goal is to be in such a love relationship with the Source of Life that our choices lead to a greater alignment with that Source. To do discernment well, we must know, deep within our soul, that God is good and desires good for us and for all of creation.

One thing I really love about the principles of discernment is that they have been developed over centuries by people seeking to be faithful. Many of the principles are based in Jewish and Christian scripture but they are also based in the lived experience of people just like us desiring a deeper relationship with God. We can be particularly grateful to two branches of the Christian tree for prolific writing about discernment—Jesuits and Quakers.

Discernment from the Jesuit Tradition

Jesuits are priests from the order founded by Ignatius of Loyola in the mid-1500's. Ignatius studied what he called "movements of the heart," both those that moved us closer to God and those that made us feel detached from God.

This study grew out of a period of convalescence in his life. As he recovered from a debilitating war injury, Ignatius noticed how he felt after reading the only books he had available to him in the convent—ones about the lives of Jesus and the saints. Prior to this injury, Ignatius enjoyed romantic writings about brave knights devoted to beautiful women of royalty. Not having those books in the convent to read, Ignatius daydreamed about romance, and noticed that when did, he would feel warmth and joy for a little while but was left later feeling "dry and dusty." And when he read about the life of the saints, he noticed that he felt a lasting peace and a desire to be like them.

Out of these reflections on his inner life, Ignatius determined that we can examine the movements of our heart for evidence of consolation—those lasting feelings of peace, joy, love and patience; or for desolation—the feelings of being dry, dull, despairing, or anxious. He taught that an examination of these inner movements (using the prayer practice of the Examen over time) can help us discern how to follow the path of life, which is the path God desires for us.

You can read Ignatius' writings in *The Spiritual Exercises* or you can find many more recent books on Ignatian-style discernment (I've listed a number in the *Topical Reading List* at the end of the book). *The Spiritual Exercises* have been helpful for many people as they sort through choices in life. Ignatian spirituality is a good place to turn if you want to learn more about discernment. It is most appreciated by people who enjoy a structured process that helps them cover all their bases.

Ignatius did not propose a discreet process for discernment but his writings have produced many elaborate processes that you can find in any of the books on Ignatian discernment. These processes center around a set of questions you apply to your overall discernment question. Here's an example of a process I adapted from classes on discernment taught by Dr. Elizabeth Liebert at San Francisco Theological Seminary.[4]

Discernment Process: Ignatian Style

- *Preparation*—Find a quiet place where you will not be disturbed and have a journal on hand where you can write your reflections or jot down your thoughts. Begin this process with a prayer, asking God to open your mind and heart. Ask for honesty of heart and inner freedom from any destructive habits.
- *Desire to follow the Spirit's lead and Indifference to all else*— Ask God to help you become open to any outcome. This doesn't mean you are uninterested in the outcome of your discernment, but it means you are willing to be surprised or changed by the process. If you feel you cannot find in yourself this place of "holy indifference" to the outcome, then be honest about that and ask for the desire to be open.
- *Frame the question*—Discernment centers around a concrete question. Name the issue you wish to discern. Questions that can be answered "yes" or "no" (as in "should I start to look for another job?") or where you can list realistic and concrete options are most helpful. Your question may change over time in discernment. Write out your question and sit with it in prayer or

meditation. Pay attention to any insight, emotion or felt body sense that arises in you.

- *Look at the practical considerations*—You need to gather as much discernment information as possible (data). Don't overlook anything! Then, list two or three options for answering your question. Make a list of "pros" and "cons" for each option. Gauge at this point which option you are leaning toward. How does this option feel after considering the "pros" and "cons" for each option? Weigh your lists. Which "pros" and which "cons" feel more important than the others? Make a tentative choice among your options to "try on" for the next step.

- *Look at your life situation*—The tentative choice you made will affect the context of your life. How will this decision affect your family? Your lifestyle? How is your circle of friends affected? How does the option fit into your personal spiritual journey? What image of God pervades as you consider this issue? What is the background history of the issue under consideration? What are the "facts at hand?" Now that you have spent some time with this option, hold it in the light of your desire to follow the leading of the Divine. Notice how free or unfree you feel as you imagine yourself pursuing this option. At this time, do you want to go back and consider other options? If so, do that now and proceed with a new tentative decision.

- *Look at your beliefs and values*—When you think about the option you have chosen, how are your personal and spiritual values honored? What "fruit of the Spirit" (Gal. 5:22) is evident? Does this choice increase your generosity, openness to others who are different, your self-esteem? Does this choice give you greater inner freedom? Does it increase your capacity to love?

- *Listen to your intuition*—Imagine your thoughts dropping

down into the center of your being and becoming very still. Listen to your breath for a few minutes. Now, allow any images to freely emerge for you. Does any image predominate? In what way does this image relate to your option? What is your gut feeling about the option you have chosen? As you ponder your option, what is your present body language? How does your body feel? Can you identify a felt sense within your body that is related to this option? After listening to your intuition, and after any images or any bodily senses have emerged, do any new options emerge?

- *Use your imagination*–Imagine yourself living out the option you are most leaning toward at the moment. Then, imagine taking a different course. Which feels most right? Which allows more freedom? In which option did your body feel relaxed and energized? If it helps, use these three tests:

1. Imagine you are very old and looking back on this decision. What will you wish you had done?
2. Imagine your best friend came to you with a similar question and was leaning toward a similar option. What would you advise?
3. Imagine you are explaining your decision to the wisest person you know. What do you imagine they would say to you?

- *Examine your consolation and desolation* — As you continue to test the option you are leaning toward, examine it to see if you are feeling more consolation or desolation:

1. *Consolation*—a mostly positive movement of the heart (even in the midst of grief or longing), an increase in

faith, hope and love, inner and lasting peace, joy, an "inner knowing" that encourages, supports and enlivens your decision. Consolation generally draws you closer to God.

2. *Desolation*—a mostly negative movement of the heart (even in the midst of good fortune or excitement), a turning away from faith, a restlessness, heaviness, anxiety, an "inner knowing" that discourages, calls into doubt, or dulls the energy around your decision. Desolation generally makes you feel far from God.

- *Make your decision*—Based on all you have experienced in the questions and tests of this process, make a decision. Notice your immediate reaction. Is it one of consolation or desolation? You may choose to not act on it right away, testing to see if your feelings and thoughts remain the same for a few days. At some point, though, you must act on faith on the decision you have made.

- *Test the decision*—How does the decision feel after taking action on it? Do you have the energy to live it out? Are you feeling more consolation or desolation? How have the people in your life, especially trusted friends or guides, responded to the decision? Do you feel closer to God or farther from God as a result of taking action on your decision? If, after testing the decision, you believe it not to be the right choice, don't panic. This is a time for ongoing discernment. Do you need to adjust your decision?

Discernment from the Quaker Tradition

The Religious Society of Friends, also known as Quakers, was founded in the mid-1600's by George Fox—a man who was tired of church-as-usual and set about roaming the English countryside seeking a direct and personal relationship with Christ. Living in a time of great social upheaval, Fox proposed an unusual and uncompromising approach to the Christian faith—through silence and paying attention to what he called "the inner light of Christ" or "that of God in each of us." For Quakers, discernment comes through prayer and meditation, waiting and listening, and testing your "leadings" in community.[5]

Quaker style discernment for the individual is less about process than about listening in silence. Spiritual directors use this style of discernment when they invite silence around a discernment question and encourage the client to wait for clarity around the question to emerge. Spiritual guides who use this method also direct honest, open-ended questions (queries) to the discerner to help them reach a place of clarity.

Quaker Clearness Committee

A clearness committee is a group convened by a person, couple or group to help them gain clarity around their discernment question. The ones seeking clarity choose who they want on this committee. The process is infused with silent prayer while the committee members gently ask simple questions prompted by the Spirit.

The process is simple but not easy. It requires far more listening than speaking; praying than probing; and a close attention to what is real, what is important and what is holy. Naturally, a clearness committee works more smoothly if everyone on it has experienced one before. But as long as everyone knows and accepts their role, follows the guidelines and agrees to approach this as a prayerful time of exploration, even first-timers can effectively do it.

Although there are specific guidelines and roles involved in clearness committee, it is a flexible process. Feel free to adapt it to fit your needs. The following process is designed for working with one focus person. However, the same guidelines would apply if working with a couple or a group.

A Clearness Committee Process[6]

Setting the Stage

Everyone in a clearness committee needs to understand the roles and responsibilities:

1. **Focus person**—this is the person seeking clearness on a question or challenge in his or her life. It could also be a couple. The focus person writes a short (1-2 pages) summary of the situation to be discerned with a concrete question about the situation noted at the top of the paper. This paper is then distributed to each person he or she has asked to be a discerner. The focus person arranges the time and place for the discernment.

2. **Discerners**—People the focus person has chosen to help with discernment. They need to understand that they are primarily on hand to listen to the situation and question at hand, pray, keep silence and, when they feel so led in their prayer, to ask *simple, direct questions* designed to help the focus person listen to the divine assistance within. Discerners agree to follow the guidelines listed below.

3. **Clerk**—One of the discerners who agrees to keep time and make sure the guidelines are being followed.

Important Guidelines for all to Follow

• Discerners and clerk are at the service of the focus person. If, at any time, the focus person does not want to answer a question, then you are not to press the focus person.

- Discerners are only to ask simple, honest and caring questions. The questions should not include statements, prefaced remarks or stories. A question should never be advice or judgment cloaked in the form of a question. It will be up to the clerk to gently intercede and ask that a question be reframed if it does not live up to this guideline.
- Discerners should not in any way try to "fix" the focus person, give advice or "set them straight" about anything.
- Discerners should take care that their questions are prompted by their prayer insights or the urging of the Spirit and not simply their curiosity.
- Discerners need to be mindful of the need for silence between questions and after the focus person has answered.
- The discerners do not give their opinion on anything—including unity—unless asked by the clerk at the appointed time or by the focus person in the short time for discerners' questions at the end.
- Everything that happens in clearness committee is to remain confidential. Only the focus person has the freedom to share what they experienced afterward. If the focus person asks a discerner for more information, then the discerner may answer. But the discerner is not to approach the focus person to say more, ask more, or reflect more on the matter.

The Process

- *When it is time for the meeting to begin,* the clerk begins by going over the guidelines to make sure everyone understands their role and responsibilities. Then, the clerk will open with a period of silence (at least 10 minutes). The clerk will signal when the silence is done and ask the focus person to begin with a summary of the situation or question.

- When the focus person has finished his or her summary, the clerk will ask for a few more minutes of silence. When that is done, the clerk opens the floor for *simple, direct and Spirit-prompted* questions from discerners.

- The clerk will ask for times of silence if the pace of the committee seems to be going too fast. Ideally, silence will surround each question and answer, giving discerners and the focus person space to think, feel and experience God's promptings.

- At the end of one hour, the clerk may choose to offer a silent stretch break of five minutes.

- At the end of 90 minutes, the clerk will ask the focus person if they have a sense that the Spirit is moving in a particular direction. The focus person may elaborate. Discerners are to merely indicate if they think the answer to the question (do we experience unity?) is "yes" or "no." Beyond this, the issue of unity is not discussed, at least not at this time.

- The clerk will ask the focus person if they, at this time, have any questions they would like to pose to any of the discerners. The discerners are to keep their answers brief and confined to the focus person's question. If the focus person wants to talk about unity (or lack thereof), he or she should bring it up. If the focus person does not bring it up, discerners need to keep silence on the matter.

- At the 2-hour point, the clerk will ask the focus person if he or she would like another clearness committee on this situation or question. The focus person may answer or may want time to think about it. If the focus person is sure that he or she wants another session, arrangements may be made for that following the close of the session.

- The clerk closes the committee time with prayer and reminds discerners of their commitment to confidentiality. The discerners turn their copies of the focus person's paper back to the focus person.

Clearness committee is a gentle, encouraging discernment practice that works best for people comfortable with silence and appreciative of having a group surround them with love and wisdom.

Read more about what Quaker educator Parker Palmer has to say about clearness committee in his book *A Hidden Wholeness: The Journey Toward an Undivided Life* (Jossey Bass, 2004). See the chapter on "Living the Questions" (129-149).

For information about how to adapt clearness committee for a group or organization, see my book *50 Ways to Pray* (Abingdon Press, 2006). Check out the Leader's Guide for facilitating a clearness committee for a group (pp. 177-179).

KEY DISCERNMENT PRINCIPLES (AND THEIR CORRESPONDING QUESTIONS)

Some people like processes and others prefer to improvise using key principles of discernment. These principles come from the Ignatian and Quaker traditions, and I've included questions that correspond to each principle.

Using these twelve principles, you may make your own process or explore a discernment question in a creative new way.

1. Discernment hinges on a concrete life question; a

choice between two or more options. *What is the question I need to discern?*

2. Discernment is steeped in prayer. *How am I praying about this question? What emerges as a result of my prayer?*

3. Good discernment listens to one's truest and deepest desires. *What is it that I most want in life? How do these options satisfy those "great desires"?*

4. To discern well, one needs to listen carefully to the "movements of the heart" in daily life. *What events, moments, decisions give me deep peace, gratitude, energy, love and joy? (consolation) What events, moments, decisions give me anxiety, chaos, despair, deadness? (desolation)*

5. Good discernment leaves the outcome open. *Can I be at peace with whatever God shows me in this discernment, regardless of outcome? If not, do I at least desire to be open to God's revelation in this matter? If the answer to that is "no," then pray for the desire to be open.*

6. It is important to be spiritually free (from fear, addiction, compulsion) in order to discern well. *What fears or blocks are getting in the way of exploring this question?*

7. To discern well, one needs a thorough knowledge of the options and practical considerations. *What are the facts surrounding the question? Whose lives are affected by these options? What are the pros and cons for each option?*

8. The options under consideration must be weighed using head, heart, and body wisdom. *Which option feels most rational to me? Which one speaks to my heart? Which option "just feels right?" As I consider this choice, what bodily senses am I experiencing?*

9. Discernment involves imagining yourself making a choice and reflecting on the future. *If I make this choice now, how might I feel, act or be in the future? What does thinking about this choice make me feel like now?*

10. A just discernment always considers how the option under consideration affects your family, community and people who are poor, forgotten and hurting. *How is my choice advancing God's reign in the world? How is my choice affecting people who have fewer choices than I?*

11. Discernment doesn't go on forever. At some point, you must take action. *As I make the choice, do I feel a sense of lasting peace? Where do I feel alive? Blocked?*

12. Good discernment is evaluated later, based on what emerges. *What has been the outcome of making this choice? Do I still feel consolation around the choice? Do I need to do more discernment?*

If you're interested in facilitating discernment, either for individuals or groups, play around with these processes and principles to see what works best for you and your clients.

If you feel you need more information about discernment, there are a number of excellent books on the subject in the *Topical Reading List* at the end of the book.

OBJECTIVES OF THE EVOCATIVE METHOD

How will we know we have been faithful to the evocative method in spiritual guidance? The truth is we may not see the fruits of our work in our clients.

The main objective is for the client to have full agency in their spiritual path. So, we don't have a goal for them. We hope for growth along the path, but we would be wise to refrain from trying to measure it.

Another objective for the spiritual guide is to withhold judgments. In the evocative method we work hard to make sure our responses harbor no bias, agenda or evaluation. When you notice judgment rearing up within you as you sit with a client, mentally release it and turn your attention back to the client's sacred story.

As they continue to tell their story, you may be surprised to find that your judgment was completely unfounded.

An example of this would be if a client shares that they are considering making a significant life change that affects many of their loved ones. From your point of view this is a mistake, and you could give several reasons why they should not do it. You may even suspect they have already made up their mind about this change. But you keep your judgment to yourself and find out in the next session that they decided not to make this change. They just needed the space you gave them to explore the option.

The reason we don't share our judgments is that *we don't know any better than they do what needs to happen.* We may think we know, but we don't. Their path is their own. Our judgments only get in the way.

As you learn the evocative method, it may be helpful to create a mission statement or a set of promises you make to the people who come to you for guidance. You don't have to give it to them unless you want to.

Think about: Your personal style, your approach, your values and the standard you want to be held to.

Here's an example:

To My Directees
We are here to explore your path together. Our understanding of the Divine may differ, but that's to be expected. The Divine loves diversity.

I promise to approach our sessions together with deep reverence and humility—praying and asking that we feel God's presence while together.

I promise to pay close attention to whatever you want to share and I will observe where, in you, I notice the Spirit may be living, moving and drawing you closer.

I promise our sessions together will center on you and how you discover your own inner wisdom. I will not give advice, nor will I try to fix or change anything about you.

I promise to lay aside judgments, opinions, biases and assumptions. You are the best judge of your life and your relationship with the Divine. I honor that.

I promise to hold your story in confidence, so that you can be sure it won't come back to you through a third person.

I promise to pray for you between sessions. And if you are so inclined to do the same for me, I will be grateful.

Thank you for the privilege of being your spiritual director.

TIMES TO BE DIRECTIVE INSTEAD OF EVOCATIVE

As helpful and safe as the evocative method is, there are times a spiritual director or guide must be more directive in order to be of the greatest service to the directee. These situations are not common; however, being prepared for them is essential.

It is most important in these cases that the spiritual director be a non-anxious presence while taking the necessary action.

Client Talks about Suicide

When a directee's story heads into territory in which they express that "life has no meaning," or "they have no energy to carry on," it is time to move gently into suicide prevention mode and ask a set of questions to determine if they are merely expressing fatigue or if they are thinking about suicide.

Don't panic. The fact that they are sharing this desolation with you is a good sign. Don't tell them you know how they feel (you don't) or that this bad feeling will pass (how could you know?). Simply do the following:

- Ask, **"Are you thinking about hurting yourself?"** Or, "Are you having thoughts of suicide? This question will let them know you take them seriously, and if they are not suicidal but just being dramatic, they can let you know that as well. In Gerald May's classic *Care of Mind/Care of Spirit,* he recommends finding out: "Are such thoughts frightening (usually a good sign) or comforting and seductive (usually a bad sign)? (p. 185)

- **If they say YES, they are thinking of suicide,** you need to launch into a set of questions that help you decide what to do next. Suicide prevention protocol centers around three pieces of information:

1. *Plan*—Have they thought about how they would hurt themselves or end their life?
2. *Means*—Do they have what they need to carry out their plan (pills, firearms, knives, etc.)?
3. *Time Set*—Do they intend to do it? Have they thought about when they would do it?

A "yes" to all three questions means you must explain to them that you are ethically bound to break confidentiality and assist them in getting psychiatric help. If there is a mental health hotline in your area, call it and explain the situation. Or you may call 9-1-1. If your client has a psychiatrist or therapist, you may certainly call them first.

A "no" to all three questions means you have some breathing room. Keep talking and continue to avoid any judgments or advice. After you've had time to talk it over, share with them the name of a mental health professional you trust for referral.

If you and the directee have a strong bond, and the situation has not gotten to a plan, means or time set, you may develop a written contract in which they promise to not take any action to harm themselves without first contacting a mental health professional. Only do this if you feel comfortable taking this step.

Client Talks about Hurting Someone Else

It is rare, but if your client is talking about assaulting or killing someone, you will need to use the same protocol as you would use for suicide. Do they have a plan? Do they have the means? Do they intend to do it? A "yes" answer to all three means you must break confidentiality and advise the authorities.

Let them know you are concerned about their anger and violent thoughts and are required by your code of ethics to report it. Again, the mental health hotline in your area will have professionals who can come to the office and provide the professional help necessary.

If the client tells you they already have been abusive to a child or elder, you must report it. More on this in the chapter on ethics.

Client is Being Abused

If you suspect your directee is a victim of domestic violence, you will want to become directive and find out:

- Are you safe?
- Is someone hurting you?
- Have you contacted a domestic violence center for help?
- What are your options for escaping this violence?

You cannot rescue a person from their situation, but you can let them know their safety is of prime importance and refer them to a domestic violence expert.

Client is Inebriated or High

Spiritual direction is not possible with a person who is heavily under the influence of drugs or alcohol. If you can tell it is useless to proceed, confront the client and let them know you will only work with them when they are sober. Regardless of how they got to your office, you are ethically bound to arrange safe transportation to their next destination (call them a taxi or call a friend to come get them.) You are under no obligation to take them anywhere.

Client is Physically Ill

Spiritual direction is not possible with a person who is clearly sick and needs to be resting at home or sent to the hospital. (Chronic illness is different—many clients come to spiritual direction despite chronic illness and no intervention is necessary.) As soon as you notice your client is unable to function and needs medical help, stop doing spiritual direction and find out what they need. If they just need to go home and rest, let them go. If they have no transportation, offer to make some calls for them. If they need emergency help, call 9-1-1. You are under no obligation to take them home or to the hospital, but you must help them get the assistance they need.

Client Seems to be Having a Mental Health Crisis

Spiritual directors are not equipped to handle severe mental health crises, so if you suspect your client is having one—hallucinating, becoming catatonic, hearing disturbing voices—call the mental health hotline in your area or 9-1-1.

If you suspect your directee is suffering from debilitating anxiety or depression while in a session with you, ask them about it. There is a chance they are already under a doctor's care for this condition and what they need is for you to sit with them in their desolation. If they are not under a doctor's care, you will want to make a referral.

There is more on this in later chapters on ethics and the differences between spiritual directors and other helping professionals. The main thing to know is that on rare occasions you may have to be quite directive, so take the time to develop a list of contact information to be used in these emergencies.

NOTES

1. See Burghardt's article, "Contemplation: A long loving look at the Real," in *Church* magazine (Winter 1989) Pp. 14-18.
2. Lecture at the Hesychia School of Spiritual Direction January 30, 2006, entitled, "Introduction to Inner Life and Religious Experience: Steps for the Journey."
3. Silence is listed as the number 1 listening tool in Chapter 5.
4. Elizabeth Liebert is co-author of *The Way of Discernment: Spiritual Practices for Decision Making.* Louisville, KY: Westminster John Knox Press, 2008.
5. Quakers have gifted the world with many fine writings about their faith. You can find inexpensive pamphlets and books galore for sale from Pendle Hill Conference Center in Wallingford, Pennsylvania (pendlehill.org). Also, check out *Quaker Writings: An Anthology, 1650-1920* from Penguin Classics. (Details in *Works Cited* at the end of the book.)
6. Parker Palmer of the Center for Courage and Renewal has a web page describing clearness committee that is the best explanation around for how Quakers do it. Find it at http://www.couragerenewal.org/clearnesscommittee/.

5

TOOLS FOR LISTENING AND RESPONDING IN SPIRITUAL DIRECTION

H ere's where we get to the nitty-gritty of the execution of spiritual direction.

As stated before, spiritual direction is, at its heart, deep listening. The director listens to what the directee wants to share and interacts with the directee with one goal in mind—paying attention to what matters most in the person's life and journey of faith.

The listening tools a spiritual director must develop in order to be effective fall into these categories:

LISTENING TOOL #1: SILENCE

Listening deeply with an open heart requires silence on the director's part—inward and outward silence.

A lot happens in moments of holy silence. We're not referring to an awkward silence, where the director appears befuddled, or the silence some people experience when they get "the angry silent treatment." It is job one for the spiritual guide to notice when a time of silence is appropriate and allow space for the directee to be quiet, pray silently or reflect inwardly. In fact, for some who use the evocative method, there is a predominance of silence in a one-hour session.

Consider silence to be a key tool for an opening into transcendence. Model it. Invite the client into it. And trust it.

LISTENING TOOL #2: BRACKETING

Bracketing is the practice of putting aside your pre-occupations and inner chatter in order to pay close attention to what the other person is saying. One visual that may help is to think of an imaginary basket sitting next to you while you are doing spiritual guidance. When a distracting thought comes to you, you place it in the imaginary basket (in your mind's eye) and return your focus to the speaker. Bracketing doesn't mean you are in denial about something important that comes up for you—you can always go back to your metaphorical basket after you are finished with your session. You are just setting it aside in order to be of service to the other person.

Some things we bracket are innocuous, like what's for dinner, or our "to do" list. Some tempt us to talk more about ourselves when we hear a part of someone's story that reminds us of our own experience. And some matters we bracket are serious enough to require the help of a more experienced spiritual guide at a later date. Those items should be pulled out of the basket right after a session, written up and taken to a spiritual direction supervisor so that you become aware of those places within you that need attention. Supervision is explained in more depth in Chapter 9 on Ethics.

LISTENING TOOL #3: NOTICING OPENINGS AND BLOCKS

The director's power of observation is a valuable skill to be developed. You are with this person to *notice* where you sense the Spirit is alive in their story. A helpful framework is to think in terms of openings and blocks.

Openings

This terminology comes from the Quaker tradition and it refers to waiting for what seems like a breakthrough or opening, from the Spirit, allowing the person to move forward or to understand more deeply. Spiritual guides need to look for two kinds of openings:

- Openings of the heart or mind within the client as they explore their own story.
- Openings in the session that have occurred because you —the director—have attended and responded well or because you have stayed out of the way of the Spirit.

Although highly subjective, most directors know openings have occurred when the directee experiences an inner freedom, insight, peace, resolution, or discovers some new discernment information.

It is only natural for the spiritual guide to hope that the client experiences many openings to the Spirit in the course of a session. However, do not hold yourself to a rigid expectation. Sometimes you will not notice when an opening has occurred, or the opening happens in the time between sessions. We hope for openings; we pray for them; we do our best to attend and respond in appropriate ways; and then we leave the rest to the Divine.

Blocks

We exist in a world full of spiritual blocks—words, actions, attitudes, experiences and misunderstandings that get in the way of our relationship with the Divine or our spiritual path. There are three kinds of blocks that happen in spiritual direction, however the most important ones for the guide are the last two.

- *Blocks within the client that hinder their spiritual progress.* Blocks are a fact of life. We collect them over time! Everyone has them and your directee is no exception. Once you notice what you believe to be a block in a directee's way, use it as information to inform your responses. Treat these blocks carefully, *allowing the client to name their own blocks and decide how to approach them in spiritual direction.* It is jarring for a guide to name a block for the client. Good spiritual directors simply notice what they suspect may be a block in the directee and consider mindfully, perhaps with their supervisor at a later time, how to help the client explore this hindrance.
- *Blocks between the client and director.* Blocks between guide and client might be personality differences, cultural differences, judgments or even conversational styles. Something between the two of you is in the way. When you notice these, it is the responsibility of the director to gently work it out. If you need to learn more about different personality types or other cultures, then do your homework. It may be helpful to bring it up in a session and find out if the directee notices it as well— just make sure you don't blame them for it! You may find the block is just too hard to overcome. For example, if you are married and your client feels your marital status is a block, then have a referral handy. Blocks like that just can't be worked around.
- *Blocks created by the director.* These are the ones we directors have control over and need to be conscious of. Directors create blocks in a session when we don't listen, give advice, push our directees in one way or another, interrupt them, argue with them, pass

judgment on them, or, heaven forbid, commit an ethical violation against them (see Chapter 9).

Most blocks created by the director are simple mistakes. We hope that they "do no harm" and move on. Sometimes bringing up the block and offering a simple apology is helpful ("I'm sorry, I should have listened more carefully right there," or "That question was a little confusing, allow me to reword it for you.") But blocks that indicate a lack of care, such as falling asleep (people tell me it's happened to them as clients) or telling someone what to do are signs the director needs a refresher course or that it's time to move on to another field of work. Blocks that violate the client's basic rights—ethical violations—not only kill the relationship, they do spiritual damage to the client.

Once you have listened, the spiritual guide needs to respond in an appropriate manner. These are the most effective responding tools.

RESPONDING TOOL #1: GENTLE PROMPTS

You can say very little and be enormously effective as a spiritual director. Gentle prompts are those conversation tools that show the directee that the director is present and wants to know more.

Here are a few useful gentle prompts to help the directee's story emerge:

- *Hmmm....* Yes it seems a bit elementary, but people are used to hearing this in conversation and it is a quick way to show that you are present but are not going to get in the way of the story.
- *I'd like to hear more about...* This is the prompt to use when the director notices a part of the story that seems significant and ripe for more exploration.
- *Highlighting an important word or phrase from their story.*

For example, if a directee says, "It's strange how I felt nothing when that happened," you reply "Strange?" or "You felt nothing?" If the directee uses a particular word several times, that's a cue for a simple, gentle prompt of this nature.

RESPONDING TOOL # 2: SUMMARIES AND PARAPHRASES

We use all the tools of active listening in spiritual direction. Restating what a person said to you is a wonderful way to demonstrate your interest and presence. The spiritual director may briefly summarize what was heard, especially after the first few minutes of the opening story in the session.

It is not necessary to repeat back everything (that would take too much time), but pick a few highlights and focus on them. If the summary is not correct, the directee has an opportunity to say more and then the director knows if he or she is on the right track.

An example of summarizing:

"As you were sharing, I noticed two areas we might explore more deeply." (Name those areas and see where the directee wants to go.)

The paraphrase is similar to the summary. Simply reflect back one concept brought up in the story but use somewhat different wording. When we repeat back what someone says verbatim, it can sound like parroting, which is awkward and not helpful.

An example of paraphrasing:

Directee: I'm having trouble settling into one spiritual practice and sticking with it.

Director: Sounds like you are looking for a spiritual practice that is a good fit for you.

RESPONDING TOOL #3: CONTEMPLATIVE LISTENING

Contemplative listening is the discipline of listening with our whole being—mind, body and spirit.[1]

For some spiritual directors, this and silence are their chief tools.

Here's the anatomy of contemplative listening for the spiritual director:

- Notice everything—words, body language, emotion.
- Bracket all interpretations, judgments, desires to fix, save or give advice.
- Be a "sounding box" to magnify the teller's experience.
- Do *not* ask questions.
- Frame a response about what you felt as you heard the teller relate his or her experience.
- You may share an observation.
- Keep responses short. We want the teller to feel freedom to go deeper into the experience.
- Resist the temptation to take the teller's experience and then springboard to your own.

It is difficult to adhere to the discipline of only offering observations and reflections and not asking questions. But it's worth it. A simple, uninterpreted observation allows the directee to stay right with the story. It's less intrusive than a question.

An example of contemplative listening:

Suppose the directee is sharing a story about the relationship with her sister and how they used to do a lot of spiritual sharing in the past. The director might respond: "I notice when you talk about your sister, your face lights up."

RESPONDING TOOL #4: THE HONEST OPEN-ENDED QUESTION

Questions are the least gentle of the attending and responding tools that a spiritual director uses. However, an appropriate short open-ended question can get to the heart of a matter quickly.

The question must be honest—meaning the director has no idea how the directee might answer. An open-ended question is one that invites a longer answer than "yes" or "no."

An example of this would be:

"How would you like to explore this matter in spiritual direction?"

Honest questions have no agenda. When we ask a leading question, we are really just giving advice couched as a question. It's not allowed in a courtroom and has no place in spiritual direction either!

An example of a leading question would be to ask a candidate for ordination:

"Wouldn't you rather stay at home and attend an online seminary?"

It is also important that the spiritual director keep questions brief. If a speech is needed before the question, then the question is not ready to be asked. Directors need to cultivate patience to wait until a question is clear within them before foisting it on the directee.

Even the briefest of questions, such as "How was that for you?" can be evocative. Much more than something like this: "That was such an interesting story—I've had similar experiences and found it hard to cope. It makes me wonder how did you cope with such a stressful situation?" Cut the fatty intro, the personal sharing and boil the question down to its bare bones for spiritual direction.

Never ask more than one question at a time. Invariably the directee will answer the second one and not remember the first. (Watch any news conference to see what happens when reporters ask three questions at once!) It's very confusing to have a set of questions thrown at you all at once.

Spiritual directors must be careful when using questions. We don't want directees to feel they are being grilled or interviewed.

Here are a few of the most helpful questions a spiritual director can ask:

- What is it that you care most about in life?
- When do you feel most fully alive? When do you feel least alive?
- How have you experienced the Divine in your life?
- How and where does God meet you?
- What do you want the Divine to do for you?
- When have you felt holy presence most acutely in your life?
- How do you know when the Divine is communicating with you?
- What is your deepest desire in life? How is the Divine present in that desire?
- In what life activities do you experience holy presence on a regular basis?
- In what activities do you feel blocked from God's presence?
- When did you first notice the Divine in your life?
- If you truly felt unconditional love and holy presence in your life today, how might your actions change?
- What event in your life changed the direction of your life?
- What are your particular spiritual gifts to the world?
- What brings you to prayer? Can you speak honestly and soulfully to the Divine? How do you do that?
- How do you feel about the communities you are a part of? Are they life-giving to you?

- What are the shared beliefs in the community you are most involved in?
- How does the Divine work in and through the communities of your life?
- Which daily activities help you tap into the life force? Which ones cut you off from that energy?
- When do you feel most connected? What can you do daily to maintain that connection?
- What gives you life?
- What invites you to move courageously beyond your limits?
- When does your life have the most meaning?
- What do you feel you need to do to strengthen your spiritual life?

WAYS TO CHECK YOURSELF

If you need help determining if you are being non-directive or evocative enough as a spiritual director, here are two ways to evaluate yourself:

Percentage Rules to Ponder

1. **The 90-10 talking rule.** In most spiritual direction sessions, the director should talk no more than 10 percent of the time with the client doing 90 percent of the talking.
2. **The 90-10 teaching rule.** If you find yourself becoming more of a teacher, more directive, more than 10 percent of the time, you need to pull back. You may be pushing your agenda on the client. Teach prayer practices or discernment principles only when the client asks for it or if you feel strongly that this teaching is necessary for the client's journey. And then, only do that 10 percent

of the time. You want 90 percent of the session to be non-directive.

3. **The 98-2 sharing rule.** The directee shares about themselves 98 percent of the time. If you are talking about yourself more than 2 percent of the session, you may be overstepping boundaries. Even if the directee begs you to share, keep the percentage low. Share only what is in the service of the client's journey. Ask yourself, "Whose needs are being served by my sharing?"

Am I Doing Spiritual Direction? A Checklist

- *Did I pray or intentionally spend time in God's presence prior to the session?* If you did, it is more likely that you were doing spiritual direction.
- *Did I consider the directee's story to be sacred? Did I listen?* If you listened and treated the story as holy ground, you were doing spiritual direction.
- *Did I bracket my distracting thoughts and refuse to air them or follow them in my mind?* If you were able to bracket, then you were acting as a spiritual director.
- *Did I really get to know the whole person? Did I ask questions important to the story?* It is difficult to do spiritual direction if you do not get to know the person. So, if you asked questions that helped you understand the person better—even if they didn't seem like spiritual questions—then you were doing spiritual direction.
- *Did I remember that the Divine sits in the (invisible) third chair in the room? Was I aware of the presence of the Holy?* This is one of the great tests of spiritual direction. If you can remember that God is the true director and you are "directing attention" to places where the Divine is being revealed, then you are doing spiritual direction.

- *Did I open and close the time in some sacred and/or symbolic way?* A time of silence, a short prayer or a way of marking that this is holy space will help both of you remember this is spiritual direction and not a casual conversation or some other form of communication.
- *Was I aware of places where the Holy may be breaking through in the life of this person across from me?* Your awareness is part of what makes it spiritual direction. Their awareness will likely grow if you pay attention to your awareness. Feel free to point out the growth or breakthrough you notice in them if they do not see it. But don't push them to believe it if they are not ready.
- *Did I notice openings and blocks?* Spiritual directors look for places where the person becomes more open to God's love and light as well as for places in the session where there were blocks to God's love and light. If you pay attention to openings and blocks you are definitely NOT doing therapy or participating in a discussion or dialogue. You are doing spiritual direction. So, spend reflection time after each session asking yourself about openings and blocks. Pray about them as well.
- *Did I let go of any and all outcomes in the session?* If you can stay open to all possibilities and not worry about what does or does not happen within the directee in any given session, then you are acting as a spiritual director. The bulk of the person's experience of God happens away from you so don't ever leave a session feeling like "nothing happened so it wasn't spiritual direction." What "happens" is not up to you. You are just a facilitator.
- *Did I remain silent when silence felt right? Did I speak when words felt necessary?* An inner awareness of your own wisdom around when to speak is part of spiritual direction.

- *Did I remember that the directee's path is his or her own?* Confusing your path with his or hers is a problem. Allowing them to walk their path at their own speed and in their own way is part of spiritual direction.

- *Did I jump to conclusions or try to "diagnose" elements of the sacred story?* Leave the diagnoses to the counselors and therapists. And leave assumptions (jumping to conclusions) aside altogether.

- *Did I fall into a "fixing" mode where I wanted to help the directee solve a problem?* Again, it is their path and their wisdom will have to work out a solution. It's between them and God. Spiritual directors help people discern by asking important and sometimes difficult questions. We help them clarify where they believe the Spirit is leading them in any given situation. But we do not problem-solve. If you feel you are slipping away from discernment and into "fixing" mode, simply pull back and BRACKET.

- *Did I fall into a "teaching" mode?* It's OK to offer a few teaching tools and tips, especially if the directee asks for them (such as asking for new ways to pray or asking about discernment processes). But if you find yourself feeling more like a teacher than a listener, pull back and return to listening. Good directors teach by example— listening well and paying attention to the "third chair" in the room, God.

And one final note, which will be taken up extensively in Chapter 9 on Ethics, you learn more about yourself as a spiritual director when you keep up with the practice of supervision. A supervisor (or peer group of spiritual directors acting as supervisors) can assist you in greater awareness of how you are functioning as a spiritual guide. They also help you remember the guidelines of the evocative method.

NOTES

1. For a short and clear explanation of contemplative listening, see Maria Tattu Bowen's chapter, "Hearing with the Heart: Contemplative Listening in the Spiritual Direction Session," found in *Sacred is the Call: Formation and Transformation in Spiritual Formation Programs*, ed. by Suzanne Buckley, Mercy Center Burlingame, pages 33-41.

6

FORMS OF SPIRITUAL DIRECTION

W hile this book will focus on one particular method of spiritual direction, the form spiritual direction can take varies widely. A trained spiritual guide may work with individuals, couples, groups or organizations.

INDIVIDUAL SESSIONS

The traditional one-on-one session is what most people think of when speaking of spiritual direction. It's two people sitting in a quiet, private space, perhaps with a candle burning on a table nearby, discussing whatever life experience the directee shares.

At the first visit, the director and person seeking direction will likely spend some time getting to know one another. After the initial "meet and greet," the spiritual director usually begins the session in a way that marks it as sacred time—hopefully in a way that is comfortable for both the director and directee. I like to invite a time of silence, asking the directee to "take as much or as little silence as you need and begin when you are ready."

When ready, the client will usually share the purpose for seeking spiritual direction. It can be as simple as wanting to have someone to check in with each month as life unfolds. Or it could be a particular life situation to explore.

Sometimes the person seeking spiritual guidance is unclear about their specific needs. In that case, the guide may ask, "What brings you to spiritual direction?" or may inquire about their spiritual background just to get the conversation going.

Once the concern, story or expectation is shared, the director will begin to sense the heart of the matter. This heart is where director and directee spend time in exploration, seeking the directee's deeper truth.

While no session is really typical, there is a flow that tends to occur in spiritual direction.

- Initial story unfolds. "I'm here to explore…"
- Director listens for places in the story that have deep emotion or significance for the client (the heart of the matter). They may ask the directee to say more about those places or may ask another related open-ended question.
- Director keeps a contemplative presence as the session proceeds and may invite pauses of silence along the way.
- Director listens for the client's language for the holy and notices any image of God presented. They may ask about those, for clarification and to get a feel for the deep beliefs and values held.
- Director notices their own internal resonance as the directee shares. The director may ask the client to reflect more on that part of the story, as resonance with the director can be a sign of spiritual energy.
- Director helps the directee clarify how they feel the Spirit is leading them to take the next step on their spiritual path.

All of this may not happen in one session, but may stretch over many months of sessions. Spiritual guides need to be patient and open-minded about the growth and development of the directee.

SPIRITUAL DIRECTION WITH COUPLES

Sometimes two people who are deeply connected (spouses, partners, housemates, close friends) will want to be in a session together. Couples' direction is helpful for two people who are open to each other's spiritual journey and want to grow together, even though their paths may be quite different.

The method used is the same as with individuals, but the director needs to take care that both people have adequate time to share. It is not a good idea for one person to observe while the other does most of the talking.

The spiritual guide may do one-on-one direction with each person for a set amount of time and then at the end allow for crosstalk. Or they may take a more organic approach, having each one share when they are ready and even interact with one another while the director listens.

For the spiritual guide, the same code of confidentiality applies with couples as with individuals. The content is not to be shared. The couple can decide for themselves if they want to keep confidentiality, keeping in mind that it could be a source of conflict if one person speaks freely of what happened in the session while the other prefers the content remain confidential.

If you plan to work with couples, make sure you work with them *together*. Meaning, do not set appointments with each of them privately. It is not considered ethical to work individually with two people who are closely related (spouses, partners, housemates, close friends). To do so places the spiritual guide in a position with a high risk of triangulation—being placed in the middle of a conflict between two people.

GROUP SPIRITUAL DIRECTION

We learn things with others that we don't learn alone or even with just one other person. Group spiritual direction is an excellent way to explore one's spiritual path in community. In group direction, people discover:

- They are not alone in their questions, doubts, or need to articulate their faith.
- While their spiritual path is unique, it may parallel the path of another from time to time.
- How God interacts with each person in varied and meaningful ways.
- How powerful it can be to have a group of people listen to their story and pray with them.

Group spiritual direction may take many forms, but it will always have at least one spiritual director present in the role of facilitator. Your group needs one person trained to guide the discussion, to help people respect one another's personal boundaries, and to be the non-anxious presence that is so helpful to spiritual growth.

In group direction, many people's sacred stories are shared. No one is an observer. Participants may be given an opportunity to offer some simple responses or questions (depending on the form of direction chosen). The guide in charge is responsible for holding the group accountable to the guidelines—no evaluating, judging, offering advice or in any way imposing one's views on another member of the group. This is to ensure emotional safety for everyone in the group.

Also regarding safety: the same rules about strict confidentiality apply to group direction as to one-on-one, with one huge difference—more people are charged with keeping confidentiality. The spiritual director needs to emphasize the importance of *not revealing anything spoken in the session to people outside the session.* That includes spouses and confidantes.

Good candidates for group spiritual direction are those who enjoy the company of others and are not shy about sharing deep feelings and spiritual experiences with others. Some people choose it for its affordability, because in group direction, participants generally pay a bit less per session than they would for one-on-one direction. The cost is spread among the participants.

While there are many good reasons to choose group direction, it is not for everyone. People who feel the need for the quiet and the privacy of one-on-one spiritual direction and those who would not feel comfortable sharing their deepest questions or experiences with more than one person may find group direction frustrating.

Group spiritual direction can take several different forms. There are two models, though, that are popular and helpful to know about. I learned them with names that sound like a Three Musketeers' motto, but you may hear them described differently.

One-for-All

This is a well-known model for introducing spiritual direction to people who may not know much about it and want to experience it with others.

In this model, the "one" in the title is the spiritual director, who spends a designated amount of time in spiritual direction with each group member, as everyone else (the "all") observes in silence. If you are not the focus person sharing your story, then you are not going to be interacting with the spiritual director or group members. The role of the "all" is to observe and pray for the person who is sharing.

The spiritual director decides, based on the number in the

group and the overall time allotted, how long each mini-session will go. Silent breaks between each person's sharing allow space for everyone to change the focus.

Because these sessions are short, there may be little interaction between the focus person and the director. It all depends on how the Spirit moves in each session and how much time is available. Timekeeping, one of the duties of the spiritual director, is very important in these one-for-all group sessions.

At the end, if there is time and if the director feels it is appropriate, the group may reflect on what was heard. Where did they feel God's presence most deeply in the sessions they observed? This is not a time for stating opinions on anything specific that someone said, but to share how participants experienced the Holy during the group experience.

One value of this model of direction is that by listening to another share their spiritual journey, we learn to respect the many ways God interacts with each of us.

All-for-One

This model requires a bit of instruction and preparation of the group before launching into a session. In this model, group members (the "all") act as spiritual guides for one member of the group (the "one," which we will again call a *focus person*). The spiritual director serves as facilitator, keeping time, making sure the focus person's story is heard and honored, and upholding important guidelines for interacting with the focus person. The focus person begins by sharing whatever is on their heart and everyone else in the group intently listens, voicing open-ended questions, observations, or non-judgmental reflections when the time is right. Everyone in the group is asked to stay attuned to the flow and be attentive to the need for appropriate silence while this process unfolds. More than one person could be the focus person at each gathering, as long as you complete one session before going to the next.

The crucial guideline for sharing with the focus person is that there is to be no attempt at *fixing, saving, advising, or "setting the focus person straight."* The spiritual director's job is to intervene if this guideline is not upheld.[1]

One benefit of this model of direction is that everyone learns valuable skills in listening and responding to another's sharing.

Leading Spiritual Practice for Groups

No matter what I'm invited to do at churches or spirituality gatherings, I'm doing it as a spiritual director, because spiritual direction is the way I've come to see and interact with the world (on my best days).

Every time a trained spiritual guide leads a group in a prayer practice or meditation, they can use their skills to help the group process what it has experienced in that prayer or meditation. They do this by asking open-ended questions, making observations about what is shared, and listening—deeply—to everything people say.

Let's say you are invited to lead a class or spirituality group in a session of contemplative prayer using the *lectio divina* (sacred reading) process. Here's how you might do this as group direction:

Simple Lectio Divina

- Prepare for prayer by helping the group relax, focus on their breathing, and get in touch with the presence of God within.
- Invite the individuals in the group to listen attentively to the reading of a short passage of scripture (a poem or

other short reading could also be used) for a word, phrase or image that invites them into prayer.

- Slowly read the passage aloud three times, pausing for about two minutes of silence in-between.
- After the third pause for silence, invite participants to consider *silently* what that word, phrase or image seems to offer them. How might the Divine be present in that word, phrase or image? Allow five more minutes of silence.
- Invite participants to share both their word (phrase or image) and its significance to them in a group discussion. Encourage a slow, contemplative pace in the sharing time.
- After everyone has shared, reflect back to the group some of what you noticed in the group discussion. Ask short, open-ended questions about how the prayer was for them. Listen carefully as they share their sacred experience.
- End with a prayer of thanksgiving for what God has granted in this reflection.

For a number of prayer and spiritual practices along with guidelines on how to lead these in a group, see my book *50 Ways to Pray: Practices from Many Traditions and Times*. There is also a list of excellent books about spiritual practice in the *Topical Reading List* at the end of this book.

ORGANIZATIONAL SPIRITUAL DIRECTION

Organizations, boards and committees also use spiritual directors. For a negotiated fee, most any group that is spiritually oriented can hire a spiritual director to lead, facilitate or organize gatherings, business meetings, retreats or sessions for prayer and discernment.

I recommend this even if there is a member of the group (say a pastor or organizational leader) with tremendous skills in leadership. Why? Every group has its own personality and every group is filled with individual personalities. Sometimes those individual personalities get in the way of what the group wants and needs to get done. It is important that everyone in the group have the freedom to fully enter the experience and feel the Spirit without having to be distracted by leading or facilitating.

Also, I've witnessed clergy trying to lead discernment processes in their own congregation. The head of staff usually has a stake in the outcome of the discernment, so that's a conflict of interest to start with. Then, he or she usually has an opinion or two about what the outcome needs to be—and with their position of power in the group, what the congregational leader says usually carries a lot of weight.

Bringing a spiritual director in to lead retreats or gatherings allows for some breathing space. The spiritual director prepares for the meeting with prayer and commitment to the chosen process. They become the essential non-anxious presence, the observer committed to God and the group but indifferent to the outcome.

It can be difficult for organizational leaders to step "onto the balcony" and see what is really going on in business meetings or gatherings. The spiritual guide reflects to the group:

- Where the energy is high and lively or where it is low and sluggish
- Where the group seems to be experiencing unity or lack of unity
- Important questions that have been overlooked
- Important questions that have been asked, but not yet fully addressed
- Places where the group got derailed from its task
- Places where some silent regrouping may be called for

- Choices that call for more prayer and discernment

Because spiritual directors are trained to listen, observe and offer ways to move the interaction deeper, one salient observation or open-ended question at the right time can make a real difference.

The organizational spiritual director may relate to the group in a number of ways. The most common are:

At the Table

In some cases, the spiritual director is invited to be at the table with the group and interact as they deem appropriate (just like the director would in a one-on-one session with an individual). They may also be asked to lead a spiritual practice at the beginning and end as well.

On the Side

Another model is to have the spiritual director sit in the room but off to the side of the group, watching the process and then giving their observations or questions at a specified time, perhaps even waiting until the end.

As Discernment Coach

Groups sometimes face a particular question—a choice, a change or perhaps even a vote—and they want the leadership of a spiritual director to discuss their options and how God's Spirit might be leading them in the matter.

A discernment coach is a non-attached, neutral party that helps clarify the questions, options and how the group feels about the choice to be made. When a spiritual director works as a discernment coach, they usually begin with some instruction around key principles of discernment. (See Chapter 4's section on discernment.) For example, one principle is that, in order to discover God's desire for us around a particular choice, we must first allow ourselves to be open to wherever God leads in that choice. A spiritual director can help the group determine how open they really are to all options, and if the answer is "not very open to one option," then they work with the group around their blocks and fears concerning the option.

A discernment coach can also offer an honest appraisal of what they notice as particular options are discussed. One example comes from a time in my life when I was considering a choice between two vocational paths. One was to work as a discernment coach and the other was to become a part-time campus minister. I believed I was more drawn to being a campus minister. It provided regular income and a chance to work with young adults, a population I enjoy. I called a friend of mine who is a gifted discernment coach and talked about both options. She said candidly: "When you talk about campus ministry, I don't hear much excitement in your voice, but when you talk about discernment work, I do." As perturbed as I was to hear that from her, I also knew she was right. Her candid observation helped clarify my path.

In my perfect world, every church board, steering committee, search committee, visioning task force and every denominational working group (at every level) would avail itself of spiritual direction in this form. There is no question that stopping to consider important questions, or praying over a choice, slows the work down in the short run (a major complaint from antsy Type-A organization leaders). But in the long run, the wisdom gained is well worth the time.

NOTES

1. Learn more about this guideline by reading Parker
   Palmer's classic article about Quaker Clearness
   Committees, found online at the Center for Courage
   and Renewal's web page on the practice:
   http://www.couragerenewal.org/clearnesscommittee/

WORKING OUTSIDE YOUR TRADITION, CULTURE AND COMFORT ZONE

W hile some spiritual directors limit themselves to working with niche populations, others want the adventure of working with people outside their spiritual tradition, culture or comfort zone. It is challenging—you need to do some research, take care with the language you use in spiritual direction and, more importantly, be open to spiritual experiences quite different from your own.

Rest assured: When we use the evocative method in spiritual guidance we can work with just about anyone. Deep and contemplative listening, being wholly present to the person in the room with us, and asking simple open-ended questions are practices valued in all religious and cultural traditions. Just stick to the basics of spiritual guidance, have no agenda for the person you are working with, and remember you are there to help the directee take the next step on *their* spiritual journey.

Just remember, it's not about you. It's all about them and the Divine.

This chapter serves as an introductory guide to working with diverse populations. It won't go into specifics about all the faiths, cultures or life situations you could encounter. But I hope it will offer some basic tips you need to work outside your comfort zone.

HOW MUCH DO I NEED TO KNOW?

Let's say you are a woman who's been working primarily with women in spiritual direction and you'd like to expand your practice and accept men as clients. Or you have been approached by a young adult but have only worked previously with older adults. Maybe you are a layperson and you get an inquiry from a clergyperson. You want to work with them, but you're nervous about how much they supposedly know about spirituality. What do you do?

- *Relax.* Remind yourself that if you use your basic skills, intuition and sensibilities learned from your spiritual direction training program, it will be enough.
- *Ask for guidance from the Divine.* Don't forget to pray! The Spirit is generous when we ask for assistance in helping others on their life journey.
- *Do some research.* The Internet and libraries are amazing places for information to help you ready yourself for working outside your comfort zone. (Make sure you check several sources on your topic so you can weed out information that is inaccurate or judgmental!)
- *Contact your supervisor.* One reason supervision is so helpful is that it offers us a confidential source for consultation. Your supervisor can help you find the peace you need to expand your practice. If they can't help you, they can assist you in finding a resource that will. (Read more about Supervision in Chapter 9 on Ethics.)

WORKING OUTSIDE YOUR RELIGIOUS OR SPIRITUAL
TRADITION

The Spirit loves diversity. Just as there are over a hundred (maybe more) Christian denominations, there are also various strains in Judaism, Buddhism, Islam, Hinduism and nature-based religions. Even if you think you know a lot about one or more of those great religions, there are probably branches you haven't encountered.

You will never know all you want to know about the religions of the world, and you don't have to be an expert in world religions to do interfaith spiritual direction.

So, imagine you are an Episcopalian spiritual director and a Hindu person contacts you for spiritual guidance (yes, it has happened!). You know very little about Hinduism, but you are interested in working with this client. Beyond the advice given in the last section, what do you need to be aware of?

- *Language.* When you have that first session and you ask "What brings you to spiritual direction?" listen carefully for the language your client uses. If they don't use a name for the Divine, ask them what language and terminology they prefer. Then use that language with them. Your research before or after the first session will alert you to the fact that Hinduism is polytheistic and your directee may have one particular god or goddess that is dear to them. Honoring a person's language for the divine is one of the most welcoming things you can do.
- *Honesty.* Be forthcoming if you don't know much about their tradition. Let them know you are interested and that you may ask some basic questions just to understand it better. That is also a welcoming practice.
- *Propriety.* You may be accustomed to opening and closing your session with a particular prayer or ritual

that means a lot to you. Don't do that on your first session and maybe not ever with some clients. Get to know *their* sacred practices first. The safest and most appropriate way to open and close a session with a directee you don't know well, and especially one from a tradition you are not familiar with, is to simply take a few moments of silence. Word prayers can be stumbling blocks. I'll never forget the time I ended a session with a Muslim and I referred to an image of God—then quickly remembered that her tradition rejects images of God. I apologized and was grateful for her understanding.

WORKING WITH CLIENTS WHO ARE A HYBRID OF TRADITIONS

The more comfortable you are with people from different religions, the more comfortable you will be with people who are on the edges of religion and spirituality.

Many spiritual seekers these days give themselves labels like:
Zen Catholic
Jewish Buddhist
Sufi Christian
Spiritual but not Religious

Perhaps they have been raised in interfaith households and have practices from more than one faith. Or they have explored a variety of traditions and are gleaning wisdom from many paths.

These spiritual seekers and hybrid believers are much maligned in the media and among people who demand orthodoxy in their traditions. They've been accused of lacking depth and narcissistically creating their own religions. One mainline pastor received a lot of media attention in a blog post a few years ago by asking them not to bore her with their rejection of institutional religion.[1]

These stereotypes are not borne out by the experience of most spiritual directors I know. Increasingly, people with no particular religious affiliation are going to spiritual direction because they've been alone in their quest and need to talk with a nonjudgmental and compassionate guide.

WORKING WITH PEOPLE WHO ARE NON-THEISTIC

There are non-theistic strands in most world religions. A non-theist is someone who rejects traditional notions of God or a Higher Power. The term non-theist covers a lot of ground—while atheists are non-theists, not all non-theists are atheists. Some adherents of nature religions believe in a creative force but not any particular god.

What distinguishes most non-theists from theists is that they do not believe in a *personal God*. Their language for the unseen world may be very different than that of a theist. They may believe in a cosmic force, spirit or intelligence, but they may not call on this force for specific help in life. Plenty of Christians, by the way, now describe themselves as non-theists. In the tradition of progressive Christianity, there are a great many who follow Jesus' teachings while stressing that they do not believe in the personhood of God (at least as humans understand personhood). You also find many Jewish people who understand God more as a creative life force than as a person.

Spiritual guidance with a non-theist usually centers on deep listening for where, in their life and experience, they feel the strongest sense of meaning or connection with a benevolent life-giving force that is both within them and beyond them.

While there are non-theist spiritual directors, a non-theist may choose a spiritual director who is a theist but open to (and certainly not judgmental toward) working with them. The challenge for the spiritual director, especially one who appreciates a personal understanding of God, is to watch the language used when responding to the non-theist's story.

For example, I frequently use short, guided meditation practices with directees in which I invite them to bring something that is troubling to them together with their favorite image for God. While theists might easily choose an image of a biblical figure or a personally meaningful image for God, the non-theist could find the exercise difficult or off-putting simply because I use the phrase "image of God," or even "image of the Divine." The exercise might work for some, if they have an image from nature such as light, wind or space.

Prayer may look very different to a non-theist—or traditional forms of prayer may not even be on their radar. Meditation may be the way they connect with something greater than themselves. I always want to know as soon as I meet them what they consider to be their spiritual practice.

Some open-ended questions useful for working with someone who has told you they are non-theistic are:

- What does being a non-theist mean to you? (Since the term can cover many religions and attitudes.)
- What spiritual or meditative practice do you enjoy regularly? What does this practice do for you?
- What do you care most about in life?
- What do you need most in life?
- What calls you beyond your limits?
- What activities in daily life are most meaningful for you?
- What activities in daily life do you find most dull or lifeless?
- What draws you to spiritual direction? What do you hope spiritual direction will do for you?
- What helps you most when you are afraid or alone?
- What is your source of strength?

- When in life are you most awake and aware?
- Do you belong to a community that feeds your spirit?
- Where do you go to catch your breath in the stress of living?

Working with non-theists in spiritual direction is rewarding. It stretches spiritual directors to be more expansive in our language and understanding of diverse theologies. It forces us to rely on the Spirit that dwells in us all—which, in the end, we need to be doing with all our directees all the time regardless of their theologies.

WORKING OUTSIDE YOUR CULTURE

Just as religious differences can be a challenge, cultural differences can as well. You can be part of the same religious tradition, say Catholic, and find that North American Catholicism differs greatly from Latin American Catholicism, Native American Catholicism or African Catholicism.

Merriam-Webster dictionary defines culture as "the customary beliefs, social forms, and material traits of a racial, religious, or social group; also, the characteristic features of everyday existence shared by people in a place or time."[2]

Ethnicities, regions, demographics, religions, institutions and families all have their own cultures. Businesses have cultures and sometimes intentionally create or transform their culture. Think of how the corporate culture of Google, with its emphasis on creativity and free-spiritedness, differs from the culture of an old-school company like General Electric.

Much of the advice given for working outside your religious tradition applies to working cross-culturally.

- *Be unassuming and open-minded about your work across*

cultures. If you aren't familiar with a topic they bring up and feel lost, ask for clarification.

- *Curb your curiosity.* It's natural to be curious about a different culture. But don't be invasive with questions specifically about it (unless they have invited you to explore that with them). You don't want your curiosity to get in the way of what they are bringing to the session.
- *Terminology is important.* Use the language they prefer for talking about their spiritual path.
- *Back up if you misspeak.* If you inadvertently say or do something that clashes with their culture, offer your regrets. And discuss the misstep. It can be a teaching moment for you as a spiritual director.
- *Stay in touch with your supervisor.* They are your confidential resource for processing how you are responding to issues of difference, diversity and culture.

WORKING OUTSIDE YOUR COMFORT ZONE

If we are being honest we have to admit that each of us has a comfort zone. And we are all outside of someone else's comfort zone! This section is designed to help you stretch, grow and consider working with a wide range of populations in spiritual direction. *Please note: I do not mean to imply that any of the populations discussed in this section are inherently uncomfortable to work with in spiritual direction.*

Two good questions for any spiritual director to ponder are:

Who do I want to work with?

Who am I anxious about or afraid to work with?

Certainly, spiritual guides have the option of deciding who they want to work with and what populations are a good fit for them. Who you want to work with indicates your comfort zone. You can try to stay in your comfort zone as a guide, but good luck with that. The Spirit has a way of gently prodding us toward expansion.[3]

Who you are fearful of working with is an indication of where you need to do some inner work, because as most experienced spiritual directors will tell you—you will be confronted at some point with a client that brings out fear and anxiety in you. These directees invite us to look at our inner shadow, those parts of ourselves we would rather not confront.

This section is designed to help you work with some populations you may be less familiar with.

Gender

No longer do two categories—male and female—suffice for talking about gender. We live in a nonbinary world, so you may want to skip down to the section on gender and sexual minorities, because in many ways we are all part of a gender and sexual minority.

However, just a few words about the traditional gender identities of male and female.

If you identify as female and want to work with people who identify as male or vice versa, you may jump right in and use the evocative method and learn about gender differences "on the job."

Another way to approach it is to prepare yourself by reading essays, books, or other media created and generated by the gender you want to work with. Men should read feminist writers and women should read male writers. Don't limit yourself to books on spirituality (although they are a good place to start) but also read theology, fiction and nonfiction books that speak to issues of gender.

Even if you do a lot of research, be cautious not to stereotype your directee. Many women have a strong masculine side and many men have a strong feminine side to their personalities. The research is for you to become more comfortable with your directee. Don't become too attached to what you learn. Directees have a way of constantly surprising us!

Gender and Sexual Minorities

Gender and Sexual minorities (GSM) is an umbrella term considered more inclusive than the long (and growing!) acronym LGBTQIA. We're talking lesbian, gay, bisexual, transgender, queer, intersex and asexual. Also included in the GSM umbrella are agender, pansexual, polyamorous, bigender, third gender, questioning, and then there are the allies who support all of the above. If you are not familiar with these terms, I highly recommend the frequently updated website itspronouncedmetrosexual.com for its comprehensive list of GSM definitions.[4]

Openness to GSM persons is crucial for spiritual directors. Gender and sexuality may be something your client wants to talk about—if they feel safe with you. On the other hand, your directee may not want to be defined by any category and may not reveal it to you at all. Talking about sexuality and gender is a personal choice and it is only a topic for discussion if and when they choose to bring it up.

Cisgender refers to a person whose self-identity conforms to the gender corresponding to their biological sex. Transgender refers to a person whose gender identity, expression or behavior is different from those typically associated with their assigned sex at birth.

As with other populations, spiritual guidance work with a GSM person is not terribly different from working with anyone in spiritual direction. Beyond using the evocative model, here are a few key principles spiritual directors need to keep in mind when working with gender and sexual minorities:

- *Know and use appropriate terminology.* It is especially

important for a straight and cisgender director to be aware of the importance of language. You don't have to know every term used to describe gender and sexuality, but a basic understanding of the fluidity and expansive nature of gender and sexuality is helpful.

- *Use the pronoun the directee prefers.* This is most important in working with transgender clients. When Bruce Jenner transitioned and became Caitlyn Jenner, it was no longer appropriate to call her Bruce or use the masculine pronoun. Some transgender and other GSM persons prefer to use the pronoun "they" instead of he or she. That may be new for you, and if so you must become comfortable with the use of they in that way.
- *Do not ask intimate questions.* This seems obvious, but sometimes people let their curiosity get the best of them. If the directee wants to talk about anything intimate, they will bring it up.
- *Know that society—especially in some religious traditions— has frequently been unkind to GSM persons.* If and when a person from a gender or sexual minority seeks you out for spiritual direction, you are blessed. Your spiritual care of them may be the only spiritual care they have received in a long time.
- *Gender identity is insistent, persistent and consistent.* It simply is what it is. If you try to change what is, or indicate in any way that you feel someone's gender identity is "off," you do great harm. Variation along the gender spectrum is to be expected because biology loves difference and diversity.
- *The coming out process can be deeply spiritual.* It is profoundly moving when a GSM shares that process with you. But keep in mind it is their story to share. There is no need for you to call attention to it before they are ready.

- *If you want to be truly open and affirming of gender and sexual minorities, make sure your marketing materials indicate that you are LGBTQ friendly.* It is important that all GSM persons who want to be in spiritual direction be able to find directors who offer safe space and a nonjudgmental presence. Make it explicit, not hidden.

The percentage of churches that are truly "open and affirming" to LGBTQ persons is small. This is not something you need to bring up in spiritual direction, but it is a reality that you need to understand.

Here are a few open-ended questions that are appropriate to ask any directee, especially someone who identifies as a gender and sexual minority.

- What have been the spiritual high points in your life? Low points?
- *If a transgender person brings up transitioning,* you might ask how their relationship with God has been through the transition.
- Has your understanding of God shifted over the years?
- Where do you find spiritual community?

It is my hope that all spiritual directors are always open and affirming of any person they encounter in direction—regardless of gender identity or sexuality. Welcome them when they show up for spiritual direction and advocate among friends and religious institutions for full inclusion.

Aging Populations

Spiritual direction is especially helpful in times of great transition, and aging brings with it many transitions. One of the most emotion-laden times in life is when a person exits a career and begins retirement. It is a rich opportunity to explore identity, new callings and spiritual gifts.

Three significant transition points for people over 55:

1. *Approaching retirement.* Young seniors considering who they are outside of a career identity. Adjustment to the idea of retiring.
2. *The first few years after retiring.* Seniors with energy, adjusting to retirement. Figuring out what to do with themselves outside of work. Searching for a mission in life.
3. *Becoming very old.* Adjusting to a decline in health, mobility and ability to live independently.

Hopefully the person on an intentional spiritual path approaches retirement mindfully—praying about the timing, discerning their way financially, and entering this new phase of life with intention. But that's not always possible. Sometimes people lose their last job and are forced into retirement earlier than they had hoped. Or their health does not permit them to carry on in the workforce. A spiritual director can help those thrust awkwardly into retirement to accept and learn from their upsetting experience.

Issues of identity— Who am I now that I'm not in the working role I had for so long? —are frequent topics brought up in spiritual direction. A spiritual guide can remind the retiree that it is helpful to look at "who I am" in the context of "whose I am." Remembering that we belong to the Source of Life during all phases of our life can help us look lovingly at who we are *now*.

Although some people make light of the transition out of a career, and may have a "take that job and shove it" attitude when they retire, others feel adrift. A spiritual director can help retirees who still have energy and desire for a good work to do discern what they are called to now. However, in my experience, directors need to understand that this discernment for the retiree seeking a new mission or call in life may take years rather than weeks or months! As our bodies slow down, the discernment around what volunteer or part-time job we are a good fit for may slow down as well. Stay at a contemplative pace with the retiree and perhaps model for the new retiree what a contemplative pace might be!

Here are a few questions or reflection points that are useful when working with retirees:

- For those considering retirement, ask them to imagine a healthy, joyful retirement and also imagine delaying retirement. Which scenario feels more life-giving to them right now?
- What do you need to know in order to retire well?
- What is drawing your attention as you adjust to retirement?
- How has your image or perception of God changed as your life situation changes?
- What do your mind, body and spirit need as you shift gears?
- How well are you now taking care of yourself? How would you like to take care of yourself now that you no longer have a work commitment?
- How are your particular spiritual gifts being used in the world now that you have more time to consider them?
- For the retiree who needs to pick up paying work to make ends meet, ask about activities that seem to transport them to an energetic state of flow. How might some of their hobbies, dreams or passions inform their choice of a part-time job? How will they remain balanced and healthy while also working? (They may want to come up with a plan or a rule-of-life about this).

And then there is the very old client whose adjustment is to a life that is far less independent than it used to be. In most other cases, the directee comes to the director's office, home or other pre-arranged location. But how do those people who are not mobile or confined to their home receive spiritual direction? The director must either visit them at a distance (phone or Skype) or come to their home.

One spiritual director I know was contracted by a family to make a weekly visit to a woman with dementia. This elderly woman had been a faithful member of church all her life. Rev. Elizabeth Lyman gave me permission to share her experience of meeting weekly with "Mary."

I would say my work with Mary is more of a spiritual companion than director. She is the widow of a pastor and has a Master's degree in Christian Education. We spend much time talking about her past since the present can be elusive. She played the violin all of her life— including second chair in an orchestra long ago. She played small concerts at the assisted living home where she resided until 3 months ago when she fell and broke the bones in her shoulder. Now she can no longer lift her arm—no longer lift the violin to its rightful place.

I think the most important time I spend with Mary is in reading and discussing Scripture. Her mind is still sharp there. I read to her from her own Bible—a well-worn one with all sorts of notes in the margins and underlined passages. I often read her notes back to her and I let her speak of what that passage meant and means. Here, in the ancient words, she is present.

I am discovering that time with Mary is liminal time. She asks if I can put a CD of Mozart in her player for her. As the music fills the room, I look over to see Mary, eyes closed, fingering the strings in her lap.[5]

When working with a homebound person, the spiritual guide needs to let go of some of the rules we learn in training programs. We might visit with them more than once a month, but it may be for less than an hour. It is acceptable to choose a sacred reading to share with them, sing an old hymn or discuss their theology.

Many of the same rules, though, do apply:

- We cannot fix anything for them.
- We must listen deeply.
- We must allow them to tell their sacred story, regardless of where it goes or how much sense it makes to us.

Some things to keep in mind when visiting a homebound person:

- *Don't overstay your welcome.* They usually don't need a long visit. I once stayed a little past an hour (not watching the clock) and noticed the person I was visiting was starting to fall asleep!
- *Simply ask, "How are you today?"* It may lead to the story they most need to tell you. Yes, it will be a lot about their aches and pains—that is their life. Listening is our greatest gift of empathy.
- *Ask about their life and history.* It can be very healing for them and quite interesting. One elderly man I visit with has been openly gay most of his life. I asked him what it was like to be gay in the 50's and 60's and he lit up with stories about where the gay culture in Phoenix was lively "back in the day."
- *If you know them to be religious, always ask if they want to pray.* Even if they are not too religious you can always ask—they will tell you their preference. Many find it comforting to have someone pray with them. The Lord's Prayer is always a good choice for Christians. Silent prayer can be effective as well.

- *If you know they are lovers of scripture, read some of their sacred texts to them.*
- *If you are aware of a hobby or talent they used to enjoy, talk about that with them.*
- *Be careful with religious language.* It may mean something different to the person you are visiting than it means in spiritual direction. I once asked an elderly woman the old Methodist spiritual question: "How is it with your soul?" I was simply asking how her heart and spirit were doing. But she thought I was asking her if her soul was in eternal jeopardy. Luckily for me, she questioned me about it and I was able to tell her I was not in any way worried about her soul. I made a mental note to save that question for Methodists or perhaps not use that question anymore.

Working with people in the second half of life is humbling. As we cross these aging thresholds, our thoughts frequently turn to mortality and life in the unseen world. Spiritual direction is the perfect place for expressing those thoughts and exploring faith.

Young Adults

Young adulthood is full of adventure and options. So much so that many young people become adrift in a sea of possibilities. If they say "yes" to one option, they are saying "no" to others, and that can be difficult. Spiritual direction, especially when it's focused on vocational discernment for young adults, can be a life raft on that sea.

There really is not a lot of difference in doing spiritual direction with young adults than with older people. The difference is how *open* the spiritual director is to someone who has grown up in a digital world, lives comfortably and closely with technology, and who may need a lot of time and patience to navigate that stormy sea of possibilities. Young adult clients need spiritual directors who are comfortable with them "trying out" a lot of different paths in order to find what's right for them. I have worked with young adults in vocational discernment who were looking at five or more possible options for graduate programs— and they wanted to do all of them! Yet as we talked about the concrete details involved in each one, new clarity would emerge.

Young adults frequently need to discern issues around relationships. Yes, there can be a lot of drama in a young person's life —remember your twenties? Compassionate spiritual directors sit with the desolation of broken relationships, questions about sexuality and gender identity, and hold space for the anxiety that a young adult may feel about finding a life partner.

Here are a few tips for doing spiritual direction with young adults:

- *Be mindful of where you do spiritual direction with young adults.* They may want to meet you at a coffee shop for a session. This has pros and cons. A public place feels comfortable for them, but for an on-going direction relationship that will involve deeper emotional waters, I recommend persuading them to meet you in a more private location, at least after that first visit. I've heard chilling stories about private conversations being overheard—and commented on by outsiders—when direction took place in public.
- *Be calm in the face of drama.* Emotions may run high. If you remain a non-anxious presence they get the message that it is just fine for them to "fall apart" in your presence. The best thing you can do is sit patiently and hold the space.
- *Appreciate their worldview.* Most millennials appreciate when spiritual direction points them toward questions of social and economic justice. They love that St.

Ignatius asks people in discernment to consider how their decision affects those who are weaker, poorer and less powerful. Questions about this are rich and fertile ground in spiritual direction.

- *Consider their financial situation.* Many young adults are deeply in debt from student loans, low-paying jobs and the high cost of living. Mention and promote your sliding scale. I'm happy to lower my rate to fit a young person's budget.

Young adults generally enjoy spiritual direction with an older adult. Still, I hope more young adults will enter spiritual direction formation and training programs. We all have a lot to learn from each other.

Persons in Recovery

Addiction recovery can be a deeply spiritual process. Whether it is addiction to alcohol, narcotics, gambling, food, sex, codependency or debt (the list can get long), accepting help from your Higher Power as you refrain from the addictive behavior can make the difference between life and death.

Spiritual directors are an important resource to an addict who wants a deeper exploration of the spiritual path they are on. In Gerald May's classic book *Addiction and Grace*, May writes "addiction exists wherever persons are internally compelled to give energy to things that are not their true desires."[6] Our job is to help people focus on and nurture those true desires.

May's definition could fit for all of us—whether we admit to our addictions or not. A spiritual director does not have to be in recovery to assist someone who is. But there are many spiritual directors who are in recovery and want to work with others in recovery. Their life experience serves them well as a comforting backdrop for the directee. Perhaps they understand addiction in ways that would be helpful for the client.

There are many ways to be in recovery. Not all persons in recovery are participating in the well-known Alcoholic Anonymous Twelve Step program, which is adapted for many different kinds of addictions.[7] However, it is helpful for *all* spiritual directors to have a passing familiarity with AA's twelve steps because as any church member knows, there are probably more people coming to a church during the week for 12-step meetings than are attending Sunday worship. And even if the person coming to direction is in a different kind of recovery program, they will probably be acquainted with 12-step language.

In fact, language about matters of the spirit may be the most noticeable difference between working with someone in recovery and someone who is not. The directee may refer to God or may use Higher Power language. They may revere the "Big Book"[8] the way some Christians revere the Bible. Some will come from a religious background, but others will have discovered spirituality solely through their 12-step meetings and will be searching for an additional spiritual tradition or community to connect with. Many people in 12-step programs come to spiritual direction wrestling with what it means to work the eleventh step, which states "we will seek through prayer and meditation to improve our conscious contact with God, as we understand God, praying only for knowledge of God's will for us and the power to carry it out."[9]

For some in recovery, identity as an alcoholic or addict is important. For others, it may be just one aspect of their life's journey. It may be a large part of the content the directee brings, or it may only come up now and then. Issues of shame, guilt and forgiveness may come forward once they trust that spiritual direction is a safe place to express and process those feelings.

Some open-ended questions for the spiritual director to consider using when working with a person in recovery:

- How have you experienced God in your recovery process? (If they have already brought up that they are in recovery.)
- How do you pray best?
- (If they identify with the twelve steps) What step are you currently working on?
- (If they use eleventh step language) How do you seek to know God's will?
- How did you understand God when you were actively using? What does Higher Power mean for you now?
- Where do you find spiritual support in community?

People in AA and other programs that emphasize Higher Power learn the importance of living their faith. This is what spiritual direction has always been about, making this relationship an important resource for the accompaniment of the recovering addict.

Persons with Physical, Mental or Emotional Disabilities

If spiritual direction is an inclusive practice it must be readily available to people who are differently abled. That means we are willing and prepared to meet with people with physical, mental or emotional disabilities.[10]

Regarding physical disabilities, make sure the location you choose to meet people in is accessible to people who use wheelchairs, walkers or canes. Before your first visit, if the prospective client has told you about a disability, find out if they have any special needs you should know about. Most likely the physical disabilities you encounter will offer challenges of decreased mobility, speech impediments, sight or hearing impairment. With the exception of those hearing-impaired persons who require communication in sign language, you can usually make small changes in the environment for accessibility.

- Be careful about rugs or other uneven floor surfaces for people with mobility challenges.
- Chairs with arms are helpful for people who have trouble standing from a seated position.
- Use enhanced lighting if your client is losing the ability to see.
- Ensure a quiet room for someone with impaired hearing. Project your voice a bit more than usual (spiritual directors sometimes lapse into a near whisper, jokingly referred to as a "spiritual voice," which is not helpful for people with hearing loss).

People who experience mental or emotional disabilities present a particular challenge to spiritual directors. We know we aren't therapists so we may wonder if we are able to work with someone whose psychological or emotional state is impaired. You may decide that you are not equipped to work with someone with a serious mental illness (SMI) such as schizophrenia, bipolar disorder, or a psychosis involving delusions. Problem is, unless the prospective client tells you ahead of time about their illness, you may not know until you are deep into spiritual direction with them.

If they tell you they have a serious mental illness, ask them if they are in treatment with a mental health professional (preferably a psychiatrist and a therapist). If they say no, the safest and most ethical response (unless you are a licensed mental health professional as well) is to tell them that you will only be their spiritual director if they are also in treatment for their illness. And, if you think it necessary, ask that they give you written permission to speak with their mental health professional so that spiritual direction and psychotherapy are not inadvertently working at cross-purposes. When you speak with the mental health provider, you may have to explain what spiritual direction is all about. Find out from the therapist what they think the client needs from conversations about spirituality. This can be a great learning experience for the spiritual director and the therapist and it ensures that the client gets harmonized care.

I have worked with several clients who told me they have a serious mental illness and were in treatment for it. In two cases I needed a consult with their therapist, which was illuminating and allowed the spiritual direction relationship to continue. Only once have I turned someone with an SMI away, and that was because the prospective client told me about a serious disorder and refused to be under the care of a psychiatrist. I explained that my expertise was in spiritual direction alone and that my code of ethics prevented me from taking on clients with serious mental illnesses unless they were in treatment.

If you want to be helpful as you turn someone down, give them the name of a spiritual director you know who is also a therapist or counselor and would be qualified to take on this client. It is always a good idea to have a list of referrals to other spiritual directors and therapists handy for times like this.

If they do not tell you they have a serious mental illness, but after working with them you suspect they may have one, this is when you need to talk with your supervisor about how to proceed with a conversation about mental health.

If, upon discussing it, the client tells you they are in treatment for a mental illness, you have some options.

- You may continue the spiritual direction relationship with little change.
- You may ask for written permission to speak with their mental health care provider.
- After having that conversation, you will have the information you need to decide whether you are able to continue working with the client.
- If you feel "in over your head" regardless of the fact that a therapist is in the picture, you will need to end the

spiritual direction relationship. Express this to them in a session and offer them referrals to other spiritual directors. This needs to be done with compassion and grace because no one wants to feel rejected by their spiritual director. Your supervisor can help you through this difficult process.

Religious Professionals

For a long time, clergy were pretty much the only people going to spiritual direction. Our client base has expanded to include people from all walks of life; however, clergy, seminarians and people discerning a call to ministry are actively encouraged to seek spiritual direction. So it's likely you will work with a religious professional, whether you are an ordained person or not.

Here are some categories you may encounter:

Clergy serving Local Congregations

We need healthy religious and spiritual leaders in our faith communities—bright, energetic ministers who embody joy and compassion and know when and how to draw appropriate boundaries. The reality is, many pastors, priests, nuns, rabbis and religious educators cope with situations that leave them drained and dry. And the very people they might feel close to and want to share their concerns with—parishioners—are the ones who, for ethical reasons, they should *never* share deep personal concerns with.

This is where ongoing spiritual direction comes in. A spiritual director can hold these troubling situations and concerns confidentially and help the clergyperson pay attention to what matters most in life and ministry.

Also, it is easy to lose awareness of God when you are busy "working for God." Awareness requires that we be still now and then. How many clergy are so busy that taking time for stillness seems impossible? Spiritual direction is a monthly reminder to savor the moments when the presence of the Divine was keenly felt and it allows time to relive those moments in a contemplative setting.

Some typical concerns clergy bring to spiritual direction include:

- Difficulties with prayer and relationship with the Divine
- A loss of motivation and passion in work
- Seeking more joy in life
- Balancing work responsibilities with responsibilities to family or interests outside the congregation
- Emotional highs and lows of being a spiritual leader
- Desire to be accountable to better self-care practices
- Secrets that are causing inner turmoil
- Challenges with physical health and healing

One of the most important services a spiritual director can offer a clergyperson is assistance with discernment—the spiritual practice of making choices in alignment with one's faith and values. Sifting and sorting through a situation, considering how the Spirit is moving in one's heart and then—at the appropriate time—making the choice and taking the action can be the material for months of direction sessions with a pastor who is experiencing distress and conflict on the job or feels it is the right time to move to a new job. (See Chapter 4 for more on discernment.)

Another way to help is to inquire about the clergyperson's self-care and spiritual practices. Health statistics for clergy are alarming—many live with chronic stress and anxiety and are prone to problems related to overwork, lack of exercise and unhealthy eating habits. There is no room in spiritual direction for shaming, but there is room to ask, "How are you taking care of yourself and your spirit?" That question can open a lot of doors for further exploration of lifestyle concerns.

The Seminarian

Seminarians have special needs because they are daily confronted with content that challenges and enriches their faith life. Many come to spiritual direction for grounding—they need one person in their life who will listen and not evaluate them but help them process what they are learning. Some seminarians have a crisis of faith during their time in graduate school. They may find professors teaching material that runs counter to what they learned about faith as a child. They may find professors and other seminarians with very different beliefs than their own. It's common for one to feel their world has been "put in a blender" at seminary.

Seminary students have stressors that other graduate students experience as well. Many are financially challenged and work part-time jobs outside of a full load of classes. With the introduction of online seminaries, it is common to find an older adult, with a family and full-time job, spending hours on their computer taking difficult seminary courses. A spiritual director can help the seminarian become more aware of their time limitations and assist as they discern which tasks need priority and which can be postponed during this busy time.

It's easy for seminarians to get focused on learning about God and lose sight of spending time in the presence of the Divine. For some people, study is a contemplative spiritual practice, but for others it's just plain hard work. And hard work, trying schedules and complicated content can start to edge out a daily prayer practice. Many seminarians say they enjoy spiritual direction because it is a monthly practice they can commit to, and they know their spiritual director will ask them about their spiritual practice. In that way, it becomes an accountability practice.

Some open-ended questions I like to ask seminarians in spiritual direction are:

- What are you learning that is most meaningful for you right now?
- What is challenging you?
- How are you staying in touch with God's presence in the midst of your studies?
- What decisions do you have to make in the next few months that we can reflect on together?
- Which activities are giving you the most life?
- Which activities are draining you?
- How is God inviting you to draw closer while you are in seminary?

Naturally, I believe all seminarians should be in spiritual direction! That's why I (and most spiritual directors) offer a sliding scale so that it doesn't become another financial burden for the student. When I was in seminary, I was lucky enough to be at an institution that trained spiritual directors so we had a lot of directors-in-training who needed directees for their internships. It was a great source of low-cost spiritual direction for any student who needed it.

If you live in an area that has a seminary and you want to work with students, make sure the Dean of Students office has your contact information so they can refer to you. In this world of online seminaries, it's likely that no matter where you live there are people going through seminary. Contacting regional offices of various denominations and religious organizations can put you in touch with people who can refer students to you.

Persons-in-Discernment

People considering a call to ordained ministry usually go

through a rather lengthy process with the institutional arm of their denomination or faith tradition. This may be called a discernment process—which in some ways it is—but it is more likely to be an evaluation of the candidate by an institutional committee or working group. Candidates in these processes are usually encouraged to do their own personal discernment of call by working with a spiritual director.

It is a beautiful thing when both candidate and ordination committee agree on the outcome. But it doesn't always happen. Discernment committees usually talk about two aspects of call to a religious vocation: the inward call that the candidate feels; and the outward call, which is the religious body agreeing that the person is, indeed, suited for ordained ministry.

The work in spiritual direction primarily focuses on the inward call, and our job is to create safe space for the candidate no matter what occurs in the course of the process.

Candidates usually fall into one of two categories:

Convinced they are called and want that call confirmed. It's great to have confidence that the Divine has issued a special call into ministry just for you. However, discernment requires that we lay aside preconceived notions or agendas and leave the outcome open. That is how we deepen in our relationship with the Holy and it gives room for new insights and revelations. Spiritual directors working with this type of candidate will want to make sure to ask critical open-ended questions to help the candidate be completely realistic and honest with themselves—and with God— about this as-yet-untested-call.

Candidates assuming this attitude usually have a harder time with their governing bodies because the people with the power to ordain are more impressed with humility than certainty. These candidates are likely to be tested with more rigor and face greater resistance. Spiritual directors will need to be patient and open-minded when listening to the candidate as they wrestle with discernment bodies.

Unsure if they are called and desire clarity and direction. Candidates sometimes go through the ordination process to find out if they are suited for ordained ministry. And frankly, that is what a good ordination process is all about. Candidates with this posture come to spiritual direction for accompaniment as they listen within themselves for clarity, insight and a leading from the Divine.

One outcome is that both the candidate and the ordaining body agree on how to proceed. If they determine together that this is truly a vocational call and the candidate is suitable and ready for ordained ministry, spiritual direction will probably be a joyful, gratitude-sharing experience. Discernment may continue after the approval for ordination as the candidate seeks suitable employment. If both the governing body and candidate agree there is not really a call or a need for ordination, then the candidate (and committee) usually feel a great deal of relief and are also grateful for the discernment process.

Another outcome is that the two parties do not come to unity around the question of call. The candidate may end up in the uncomfortable position of opting out of the ordination process when the governing body wishes they would continue. Governing bodies are made up of people—lay and clergy—who, like many people in relationships, tend to want what they cannot have! Or the candidate may end the process feeling a deep call only to find the ordaining body is not in agreement.

Anytime there is not agreement in discernment around ordination, you can expect anguish and hurt feelings. The spiritual director to the candidate needs to be experienced and comfortable with holding space for their client's sadness, anger or mixed emotions, knowing there is nothing we can do to fix the uncomfortable situation.

When working with ordination candidates, it is helpful to have access to the governing body's written material on the process for ordination. How does this body understand discernment? What are they looking for in a candidate? Denominations and faith traditions have a variety of understandings of call, discernment and the purpose for being ordained. In some traditions, ordination is tied to function alone—what the ordained person is allowed to do that the layperson is not. Examples could be officiating at communion; wearing vestments; offering pastoral counseling. Other traditions see ordination as a mystical sacrament—a visible sign of invisible grace.

In addition to the information provided by the directee, one of the best resources on discerning call in community is the book *Listening Hearts: Discerning Call in Community*. Written after a long discernment process by a working group of mostly Episcopalians (lay and clergy), this book defines and explains Christian spiritual discernment in general and has excellent appendices with specific questions and reflection points for the ordination candidate. It would be well worth any spiritual director's time to read that book when working with a candidate for ordination.[11]

Warning!

Under no circumstance should the spiritual director reveal information from their confidential meetings with the candidate to a discernment body. No matter how hard the governing body tries to get you to comment, it is unethical to do so without express permission from the directee. And even with that, I'd lean toward giving less information rather than more.

The candidate may ask you for a letter of reference. If you feel comfortable doing that, proceed. I personally only write letters of *recommendation* for anyone who asks (be it a directee or student I'm working with). In this case I live by the rule "if you can't say something nice, don't say anything at all." You can easily turn down the request for a reference by saying you wish to stay out of the candidate's process beyond the one-on-one guidance you are offering.

No matter how unfair you believe the candidate's process to be, under no circumstance should you offer or attempt to intervene for them with the governing body's ordination committee. That falls under the ethical violation of meddling. After all, you are only hearing one side of the story. You aren't privy to crucial information the committee may have.

Specialized Ministers

Chaplains, campus ministers, denominational leaders, pastoral counselors, and spiritual directors are all ministers with a specialty and their needs in spiritual direction are specialized as well. Some are ordained clergy who have transitioned from local congregation work to their specialty. Some (like me) have only worked in their specialty. Some work regular hours, some are on call and others make their own schedule. Most find themselves in need of spiritual guidance either as a regular practice or during times of transition or difficulty.

Specialized ministers tend to be sensitive, hard-working people who hold a lot of people's confidential stories. Their needs differ from the traditional pulpit-filling pastor. Here are some content areas that come up for exploration in spiritual direction:

Processing emotions they encounter. Chaplains in particular are ministers who serve people in times of crisis. Hospital, hospice, nursing home or first-responder chaplains come face-to-face with traumatic events, suffering and death. In the best-case scenario, these ministers will have had excellent Clinical Pastoral Education (CPE), a rigorous education process with supervision that helps chaplains confront their feelings about the work they are doing. CPE is required for most chaplain positions, but not all. Even with a strong background in how to process difficult feelings of sadness, fear and anger, many chaplains find monthly sessions of spiritual direction helpful. Since the session is confidential, this is a place where the chaplain can explore what they have learned in CPE and find support, prayer and encouragement. Other specialized ministers may not have had the benefit of CPE and may find spiritual direction one of their only outlets for processing difficult emotions.

Campus ministers and denominational leaders in particular are first responders to a number of highly volatile situations. And while pastoral counselors and spiritual directors are usually in supervision for the inward look at their responses to their own feelings, it is highly recommended (*mandatory* for spiritual directors) that they be in spiritual direction as well.

Status within their religious denomination. With the exception of the denominational leader (who is usually quite fine with their status!), many specialized ministers feel marginalized among their peers. One former hospice chaplain I know stopped going to denominational meetings because the sign-in sheet only had one category—*church you serve.* Even after repeatedly pointing this out to denominational leaders, the sheet never changed. Some specialized ministers are ordained but others cannot be ordained because their denominations do not yet ordain women or LGBTQ persons. That feeling of being a second-class citizen within your profession is appropriate material for exploration in spiritual direction.

Difficulties working within their systems. Specialized ministers who are hired by organizations must do their job within the confines of a system with rules and regulations that take up a lot of time and have little to do with ministry. As soon as the government allowed Medicare funds to pay for spiritual care in hospice, those chaplains had a lot more paperwork on their hands. Some systems understand spiritual care but others do not. Specialized ministers who work within systems that "just don't get it" will find spiritual direction a safe place to release some of their frustration and take a look at how God manages to break through even the toughest of systems.

Shrinking job market. As the size of religious institutions shrink, you would think the need for chaplains would increase. But positions for chaplains are also waning. Denominations are consolidating their systems so that fewer denominational leaders are needed. Many colleges have no campus minister. So specialized ministers, many of whom are sole proprietors who freelance, live and work in an uncertain economy. They need the kind of prayerful "long, loving look at the real" that spiritual direction provides.

Maintaining a work-life balance. On-call work is difficult. You must be accessible at a moment's notice, even at times your friends and family need you. Specialized ministers who accept jobs that include on-call periods have to work harder to keep their life in balance. There will, in fact, be times their life is not in balance. Spiritual direction can help a chaplain or campus minister figure out how to recalibrate and live peacefully with the on-call status during those off-balance times.

Here are some good open-ended questions to use when working with specialized ministers:

- What is most meaningful about the work you do?
- What is least meaningful and in need of a change?
- How do you process your sadness or other difficult feelings on the job?
- (If they had CPE) What are some of the concepts you learned in CPE for staying balanced on the job?
- How is life for you outside of work?
- How do you take care of yourself?
- What spiritual practices help you the most?
- Where do you find spiritual community?
- What are your most meaningful connections with your denomination or governing bodies?
- When is your sabbath (break from all work) and how do you observe it?

As mentioned before, anyone giving spiritual direction needs to be receiving it as well. Spiritual direction and supervision are ethically mandatory and spiritually necessary for us. Don't neglect it just because you have a lot of spiritual friends and feel they are meeting your need for guidance. You need the confidentiality and boundaries found in regular, monthly spiritual direction and periodic supervision.

CONCLUSION

This chapter could go on endlessly listing populations and professions that spiritual directors could work with. My goal here is to write about the ones that most frequently show up for spiritual direction.

If you want to read more about working with specific populations in spiritual direction, the best resource available is *Presence,* the professional journal published by Spiritual Directors International. In almost every issue there is an article about working with particular populations.

To receive *Presence*, you must purchase an annual membership in SDI.[12]

Also, citations for books mentioned in this chapter and other resources to help you prepare for some of the populations you want to work with are included in the final chapter under *Topical Reading List.*

NOTES

1. See Rev. Lillian Daniel's essay "Spiritual but not Religious? Please Stop Boring Me." Found online from the Huffington Post at http://www.huffingtonpost.com/lillian-daniel/spiritual-but-not-religio_b_959216.html. She

later expanded the concept in her book, *When "Spiritual but Not Religious" Is Not Enough: Seeing God in Surprising Places, Even the Church*, from Jericho Books.

2. https://www.merriam-webster.com/dictionary/culture

3. I am not at all saying spiritual directors need to suffer by making ourselves available to everyone under the sun. I'm not even a big fan of the popular motto "life begins outside your comfort zone." Some highly sensitive people find it hard to be comfortable *even in their comfort zone!* If you are one of these (as I am) then a good metaphor is what yoga teachers emphasize about stretching. They tell us to stretch to the edge of our discomfort, go a little past that, hold it (stop if it's painful!) and then each time you stretch, you will grow a little more flexible.

4. Found online at http://itspronouncedmetrosexual.com/2013/01/a-comprehensive-list-of-lgbtq-term-definitions/.

5. Personal conversation online with Rev. Elizabeth Lyman, July 14, 2016.

6. p. 14.

7. For information about Alcoholics Anonymous, go to www.aa.org.

8. The Big Book includes detailed information on the twelve steps as well as personal stories of people in recovery. Find information about the Big Book at AA's website. *Alcoholics Anonymous, 4th Edition*. New York: A.A. World Services, 2001.

9. Another helpful website is www.recovery.org, which has a page for each of the twelve steps. This quote can be found online at http://www.recovery.org/topics/step-11-aa/.

10. Chapter 4 addressed how to be more directive in cases of physical, mental or emotional emergencies. This

section assumes the person you would be working with is not in an emergency situation.

11. While this book does employ explicitly Christian language and theology, it remains an excellent book on discernment in general and I believe could be used in interfaith spiritual direction as a helpful resource for the director.

12. The website for joining SDI is www.sdiworld.org.

8

HOW SPIRITUAL DIRECTION DIFFERS FROM OTHER HELPING RELATIONSHIPS

There are many modes of personal guidance and spiritual help available. People are naturally curious about how spiritual direction differs from mental health counseling, pastoral counseling, life coaching, spiritual life coaching or spiritual friendship. How does a visit with a spiritual director vary from a talk with a pastor, rabbi or imam? How is it different from meeting with a chaplain?

All of this, of course, depends on the spiritual guide and how they approach their work. For example, some spiritual directors are also energy healers and may combine the two modes in their practice. Some people licensed by a state to do mental health counseling or therapy are comfortable talking about spirituality and may use some of the tools as a spiritual director.

So, the answer to the question "How is spiritual direction different from...?" is complex and important.

MENTAL HEALTH COUNSELING

Spiritual direction can be therapeutic, but it's not the same as therapy.

Both new and experienced spiritual directors tend to worry that they are inadvertently slipping into the role of "armchair therapist," a role directors avoid—one, because to do so without a license is illegal; and two, we simply aren't qualified or educated in that area (the exception being those directors who are also licensed therapists).

The worry is not completely unfounded but can be overblown by aspiring directors. If we adhere to the non-directive, evocative method as outlined in Chapter 4 and use the tools described in Chapter 5, we will not be doing therapy.

The best advice? Stay attuned and committed to connection with the Divine and you will be doing spiritual direction. Even when a spiritual director asks the same question as a therapist, such as "How is that for you?" the director's intent is to help the client connect with Spirit, which is probably not what the therapist would intend.

If someone needs therapy, spiritual direction alone is inadequate. A person who tries to use spiritual direction as a substitute for therapy will only be discouraged. By the same token, a person who chooses therapy alone in order to explore their spiritual path might also be disappointed. Directors are not trained to help change behaviors or understand the psyche. Good spiritual directors should know a bit about psychology, but it's usually just enough to know when we are out of our league.

Some people are in both therapy and spiritual direction. Having a therapist who is interested in spirituality and willing to work in connection with a spiritual director (as I do) is an ideal situation.

Here are a few ways we can tell spiritual direction from counseling:

1. *Spiritual directors are not diagnosing anything.* In therapy, the diagnosis is crucial and can be the central purpose.
2. *Spiritual directors are not about fixing anything.* Therapists

or counselors work with the intention of helping a person change some behavior or attitude. People usually go to therapists because they sense a problem they want to solve. They may also go to a spiritual director because they sense a spiritual dilemma or challenge, but the director will not focus on solving that dilemma—we will rely on the directee and the Spirit to do that work. The spiritual director may help the person focus on strengthening spiritual practices and a change in behavior may follow, but directors don't go into a session with that agenda.

3. *Spiritual direction always has a spiritual component.* It is primarily focused on the sacred. Therapy is not. While most spiritual directors believe all of life is sacred and don't draw a distinction between sacred and secular, that distinction is useful for helping us notice the difference between the two relationships. Talking about transcendence, mystery, meaning and unseen realities are expected in a spiritual guidance relationship. In therapy, there may be a spiritual component, but that is not the primary focus. And many therapists are cautious about moving into spiritual territory. For instance, if a therapist suggests praying with a client and that client files a complaint, the therapist could lose his or her status with insurance companies.

4. *Spiritual direction recognizes the "third chair."* Directors look to the Divine as the primary actor in the relationship. Therapy is just between the client and therapist.

5. *Spiritual direction is usually less directive than therapy.* Some therapies are quite confrontational, with therapists giving a lot of advice.

6. *Spiritual directors do not focus on a person's personality structure.* Personality changes may occur as a result of

spiritual direction, but there is no expectation of that happening.

7. *Health insurance does not cover spiritual direction.* Mental health counseling may be covered by insurance; however, a growing number of counselors are choosing to not take insurance.

8. *Spiritual direction ordinarily occurs only once a month.* Therapists may want to see their clients weekly or biweekly. Spiritual directors encourage the once-a-month model so that the time together is a gentle check-in around the many experiences that have occurred over the month between sessions.

9. *Spiritual direction sessions frequently begin with some sacred or symbolic ritual,* such as prayer, silence, the lighting of a candle, the sound of a chime, etc. Counseling usually does not.

How are spiritual guides similar to counselors?

1. We both value and hope for insight on the part of our clients in a session.
2. We both deeply listen to people's life stories.
3. We both appreciate silence and what can happen in the midst of it.
4. We both refer our clients out if we believe they need a different or additional helping practice for their growth.
5. We both seek to ask questions that get to the heart of the matter.
6. We both value awareness and mindfulness.
7. We both generally spend fifty minutes to one hour in a session with clients.
8. We both hold our clients' material in confidence.

PASTORAL COUNSELING OR SPIRITUAL COUNSELING

A licensed counselor specially trained to assist clients in working on life problems and situations from a spiritual or religious perspective is called a pastoral counselor. Many times they are an ordained minister, rabbi or imam who has specialized in counseling. They may use the same tools a spiritual director uses, but will additionally be diagnosing, problem-solving and helping the client with behavioral change. A pastoral counselor may also diagnose and work with people who have personality disorders.

A spiritual counselor would be similar to a pastoral counselor —trained and licensed in counseling—but might use the language of spirituality rather than the language of a particular faith tradition.

Many people go to a pastoral or spiritual counselor for the same reasons they would go to a traditional counselor, but feel more comfortable talking with someone who has religious training or background. A person may also seek out a pastoral counselor to talk about theological issues they are grappling with.

There are subsets of pastoral counseling, such as Christian counseling and biblical counseling, which tend to focus on counseling with an eye toward helping the person be a better (more orthodox) Christian. Some of these Christian or Biblical counselors are open to a variety of theologies and others are more rigid in their theology.

Pastoral counselors are different from spiritual directors in the same way traditional therapists are different. (See the above list for the difference between spiritual direction and counseling.) Our similarity is that we both put an emphasis on the Divine and as such we may both start and end sessions in some sacred or symbolic way.

LIFE COACHES OF MANY VARIETIES, INCLUDING SPIRITUAL

Life coaching has exploded as a helping profession in the last ten years. You can find a life coach that focuses on leadership, business, health, mindfulness and spirituality, just to name a few. Life coaches are usually excellent listeners, teachers and cheerleaders for their clients.

A coach focuses on helping a person identify the goals they want to work toward, create an action plan, clear out personal blocks to success, and move steadily toward achievement. A coach will encourage you along the way and show you how to make decisions that line up with your goals.

Some differences between a coach and a spiritual guide:

1. *Spiritual directors do not have goal-setting as an agenda.* If a directee wants to talk about goals, that's fine. It's just that directors have only one real goal—to help the client take the next step on their spiritual journey.

2. *Spiritual directors may encourage directees now and then, but we do much less "cheerleading" than a coach might.* Deep and holy listening is usually encouragement enough. When spiritual directors offer too much praise, we may find our directees trying too hard to get our approval— a situation we want to avoid.

3. *Spiritual direction is not focused on increased productivity* or the development of action plans.

4. *Spiritual direction usually happens once a month and lasts about an hour per session.* Coaching works on a schedule either set up by the coach or determined by the coach and client. Many coaches meet several times a month for a few minutes as check-ins after goals have been set.

Similarities between spiritual direction and coaching:

1. We both listen deeply to our clients.
2. We both value and hope for insight on the client's part.
3. We both avoid giving advice or finding ways to fix our client's problems. Even though a coach works on goals, the coach does not set the goals for their client.
4. Spiritual directors and spiritual life coaches both place emphasis on the sacred. Some spiritual directors are also trained as spiritual life coaches and may combine elements of both helping relationships in one session.

SPIRITUAL FRIENDSHIPS

We all need people we can share deeply with—friends. But friends are not spiritual directors.

A spiritual friendship is hard to define because it's whatever the two people who enter into it decide it will be. It could involve regular meetings with agreed-upon guidelines. Or it could be a casual no-holds-barred conversation that focuses on the spiritual path.

You may be wondering why anyone who has a good spiritual friend would want or need a spiritual director. As a person who has had both—spiritual friends and directors—I can say with confidence that the relationships are very different.

Friends care deeply about us. They may even worry about us at times. Friends sometimes have trouble being neutral or with-holding opinions about the choices we face. While we want to be around someone who cares about our concerns, we may not always want to share deeply with someone who feels invested in our choices.

Spiritual directors are not supposed to have such investments. We give directees the freedom to feel what they feel and choose as they feel God is leading them. A spiritual friend may be helpful in that way, but because you already have the relationship of friend in the mix, they may have trouble resisting the urge to give advice. Spiritual directors provide the neutrality that comes from the boundaries inherent in the spiritual direction relationship.

Spiritual friendship is a peer relationship. Usually when someone speaks of a spiritual friend they mean someone they can pray with as well as talk to about spirituality. The spiritual direction relationship is not a peer relationship. It may be friendly, but the director is not technically a friend in the widest sense of the word.

The *Code of Ethics for Spiritual Directors* makes it clear that there is a power dynamic in spiritual direction that cannot be ignored. Because the directee shares a lot of personal information and the director primarily listens and observes, the director is in a role that holds some power and therefore is responsible for keeping boundaries in the relationship safe and clear. Also, most spiritual directors have training in the art of spiritual guidance. They have spent time and money learning how to be in a healthy working relationship with you. They have been schooled in the importance of confidentiality.

The main differences between spiritual direction and spiritual friendship:

1. *Spiritual direction is a formal relationship with clear boundaries and focus.* A spiritual friendship is usually casual, peer-to-peer, and does not involve a power dynamic. Its focus is whatever the two friends determine it to be.
2. *Spiritual direction is bound by a code of ethics that discourages dual relationships (wearing more than one hat with a person) and demands confidentiality.* Friends may have several roles with one another. Confidentiality could be agreed to, but cannot be assumed.
3. *Spiritual directors usually charge a fee for services.* Spiritual friends do not.

Some similarities:

1. We both care deeply for the other person's spiritual well-being.
2. We both pay attention to the sacred in the life of the one who is sharing.
3. Prayer and sacred symbolism may be involved in both relationships.

SESSIONS WITH CLERGY

Meeting regularly with a spiritual director is also different from appointments someone might make with a pastor, rabbi, imam or other spiritual leader. For the sake of brevity, let's call all these people clergy (whether ordained or not).

Certainly, you may visit a clergyperson for spiritual guidance. But they probably won't be able to spend large amounts of time over many months working with you. Most clergy are busy leading their congregations in worship, offering pastoral care to the ill and suffering, and representing the spiritual community to the world at large.

Most clergy are trained to give only three counseling or guidance sessions before they refer their congregant out to the appropriate professional—be it therapist, teacher or spiritual director. Many spiritual directors receive clients from these clergy referrals because directors are able to meet with people over a longer period of time.

The work done with a spiritual director may be more beneficial, primarily because there is no prior or dual relationship with the client. Meeting with your own clergyperson for spiritual guidance doesn't cost you anything, but because you have a relationship with that clergy, there is a greater likelihood that the guidance relationship can go off track. Think of it this way: your community's spiritual leader probably has hopes, dreams and plans for you and the community. Both of you could find the mixing of relationships messy.

It is for this reason that some (not all) clergy who are trained as spiritual directors will not take on clients from their own congregation. Instead, they will refer their congregants to a spiritual director not connected to their faith community. This is baffling to many congregants. However, good boundaries make for good spiritual guidance. More on this in Chapter 9 on Ethics.

Some differences between sessions with clergy and spiritual direction:

1. *Spiritual directors are bound by a code of ethics that requires us to have no prior agenda for the client.* Clergy are— almost by definition—persuaders of the faith. Their agenda is usually a deepening in one particular faith, that of the community they serve.
2. *Spiritual directors may or may not be trained in a particular theology.* Clergy almost always are.
3. *Spiritual directors usually remain in their one role with a client to keep interactions clean.* Clergy have to wear many different hats with the members of their community.

Some similarities:

1. Both clergy and spiritual directors care deeply for the well-being of the person they are working with.
2. We both pay attention to the sacred and value a person's sacred story.
3. Both clergy and spiritual directors refer clients to other professionals when necessary.

OTHER SPIRITUAL CARE RELATIONSHIPS

The field of the "professionally spiritual" continues to grow—exponentially! Some spiritual services are as individual as the person offering them. There are too many modes of spiritual healing to mention. Some look similar to spiritual direction and others are completely different.

The role of chaplain may include deep listening that is similar to spiritual direction. A chaplain is a spiritual representative working (or volunteering) for an institution such as a private chapel, hospital, hospice, branch of the military, a prison, a business or corporation, or working with first responders such as firefighters, police and rescue workers. Chaplains offer the ministry of presence to people in these institutions. They listen, support, encourage and sometimes lead non-sectarian worship services or memorials. A chaplain is someone to talk to about faith but he or she usually would not be available on a regular basis (unless that chaplain was also a spiritual director on the side). While I haven't yet heard of people billing themselves as "private chaplains for hire to individuals," it very well could exist.

In some Christian denominations discipleship mentors are popular. This role is quite different from that of a spiritual director. A mentor often gives advice and offers their own experience as guidance. And discipleship by definition is learning about the faith and becoming more devout.

FINAL NOTE

All the helping relationships listed in this chapter have their place, and it's important for both those seeking spiritual guidance and those giving it to be aware of what's out there. It's equally important to remember that spiritual direction is a distinct and different type of helping relationship. People may choose to combine modes, but they need to be clear with clients about exactly what they are doing and why they are calling it spiritual direction.

NOTES

1. Thanks to Jami Parrish, a counselor and spiritual director, for outlining these differences in a handout used at the Hesychia School of Spiritual Direction in Tucson.

9

ETHICS IN SPIRITUAL DIRECTION

When it comes to ethics, spiritual directors are like other healers. Our motto is "above all, do no harm."

It is an honor and a sacred responsibility to be someone's spiritual companion. It means they are trusting you with their inmost thoughts, feelings and beliefs.

Good spiritual directors live by a code of ethics, not because we are legally accountable to a certifying board—we are not—but because it's the right thing to do.

Two documents on ethics for spiritual directors are the primary resources for this chapter:

A Code of Ethics for Spiritual Directors is a short, inexpensive booklet from Dove Publications developed in the early 1990's by spiritual directors who were also working in confidential helping professions such as social work, therapy, pastoral counseling and pastoral ministry.[1] It is used by most, if not all, spiritual direction training programs and should be in the library of anyone working as a spiritual director, guide or companion. As a reference on ethics and boundaries, it is unsurpassed.

This booklet is also helpful for people receiving spiritual direction because it describes the practice of spiritual direction and outlines a directee's rights, as well as the responsibilities spiritual directors hold when they enter into this relationship. Perusing this booklet gives everyone a better understanding of the necessary boundaries on the relationship.

Spiritual Directors International Guidelines for Ethical Conduct, a pamphlet to purchase or view free online from Spiritual Directors International, the best known global learning community for the support of spiritual directors.[2] This booklet is written in outline form and is very clear and concise.

BOUNDARY SETTING

The most important ethical consideration in spiritual direction is the observation of healthy boundaries—that distance everyone needs between themselves and others.

We all attend daily to physical boundaries such as touch, doors for privacy and even how close to stand to another person. We also attend to emotional boundaries such as being true to ourselves, deciding how vulnerable to be with another person, making sure we are not pushing ourselves too hard, and allowing our true feelings to be expressed.

A boundary is like a fence we build for ourselves. We alone decide when to open that gate to another person. No barging in, jumping over or tearing down of that fence is allowed. People with firm boundaries may not open their gate as often as people with softer boundaries.

Spiritual directors need firm boundaries around our work with clients because of the natural power dynamics of the relationship. The fact that our clients share their sacred stories with us, while we do not, creates a vulnerability in the client. The more powerful person always has more responsibility to set, honor and respect boundaries.

Important Boundaries in Spiritual Guidance

Know the limits of the relationship. Spiritual direction is different from many other helping professions, and we are clear as to how it differs (see Chapter 8 for more on this). Spiritual guides must always keep in mind that our role is to assist the client in reflecting on their spiritual path and any steps they desire to take on it. The sessions are not about the director, nor are they occasions for the director to give advice or counsel.

Avoid dual or multiple relationships. Spiritual directors ensure that the relationship with our clients is "clean," meaning we avoid the complications that come from being in more than one role with our client. Directees should not be close friends, family members, business partners or students of the director. In situations where dual relationships are nearly impossible to avoid, such as in small towns or within spiritual communities, it is best to acknowledge the mixed roles, talk about them openly and agree on what is necessary for the spiritual direction relationship to feel uncompromised.

Decide who we work with. Some of us are all-inclusive—inviting anyone interested in spiritual direction to give it a try with us. Others limit our practice according to interests, abilities and schedule.

Confidentiality and mandated reporting. Spiritual guides maintain the boundary of confidentiality. What clients tell us is sacred and must not be shared. Even when taking material from a session to supervision, the director should never divulge the identity or reveal identifying characteristics of their client. No written materials about clients should get into the hands of anyone other than the director. There are instances in which spiritual directors are mandated reporters of child abuse, elder abuse and physical harm to self or others. It is best to disclose early on any legal requirements about your responsibility in reporting those situations to the proper authorities. Different states have different laws about mandated reporting. Even if your state does not require a spiritual director to report instances of abuse, it is ethical to do so.

A good rule of thumb in mandated reporting is that a spiritual director should do whatever an ordained minister or therapist in their state is required to do.

Physical boundaries. Personal space must be carefully maintained. Touching is ordinarily to be avoided—especially touch initiated by the spiritual guide. Sexual intimacy is never appropriate. The only appropriate touch for a director to initiate would be a handshake. The *Code of Ethics* advises any spiritual guide who wants to offer hugs or hold hands for prayer to examine their motives.[3] "Whose needs are being met here?" is a boundary question worth asking in these situations.

Length and cost of sessions. Spiritual direction is usually 50 minutes to an hour long unless otherwise indicated. When that time is up, the session ends, so that others may have their sessions begin on time. Even if the director doesn't have another session coming up, it is wise to honor the time boundary for continuity. The cost of sessions varies regionally and there is no formal agreement among directors within regions about the appropriate rate. A few spiritual directors do not charge anything, others ask for a donation, but most offer a sliding scale fee so that people at all income levels may have the opportunity to be in spiritual direction. (More on this in Chapter 11.)

Contact outside of sessions. There is no hard and fast rule about this, but it is wise for spiritual directors to have a sense of how available they intend to be between sessions. Some will accept the occasional short phone call, but will ask that a new session be booked if the matter takes more than 15 minutes or so to discuss by phone. Similarly, directors must let go of the directee between sessions. Praying for them is expected, but checking in with them frequently on email, phone or text is not. Whenever either party feels a pressing need to go outside the direction relationship, it is time for a frank and open talk about it.

BASIC RESPONSIBILITIES OF A SPIRITUAL DIRECTOR

Being present as someone bears their soul and expresses their vulnerability is a privilege that comes with a lot of responsibility. Spiritual directors must, at all times, keep the well-being of the client in mind.

It is the responsibility of the spiritual guide to:

Be trained in the art of spiritual direction. Even though there is no standard certification for spiritual directors, no one should begin practicing the art without proper training.

Present spiritual direction appropriately. This is the one area where directors function as teachers. Many people don't know much about spiritual direction, so it is incumbent on us to fully explain the nature of the practice, including the role of the spiritual guide (and how it may differ from other helping relationships they have encountered), the expectation that the client's story and how it connects with their spirituality will be the central focus of a session, how often sessions will take place, how long each session will be, and how each session will be compensated.

Be in spiritual direction and working with a supervisor. It should go without saying, but sometimes hubris sets in and spiritual guides forget they need that one hour a month with a spiritual director to reflect on their spiritual path, too. Supervision, which will be addressed in more detail in its own upcoming section of this chapter, is the best accountability and continuing education exercise known to spiritual directors. The *Code of Ethics* makes it clear that supervision is ethically mandatory.

Know your limitations and honor them. A good spiritual director is self-aware, constantly attends to their own inner work, and takes care to remain healthy and clear-headed. How many clients to take on, how many to see in one day, and when to take breaks from work are important matters for spiritual directors to think through as they set up their practice. As one gains experience those limitations may change, but the need for constant self-evaluation remains.

Maintain excellent care of yourself. Practice self-compassion, take time away from work, attend to your regular spiritual practice, connect with a spiritual community, treat your body to exercise and nutritious food, treat your mind to meditation, and have some fun. In many ways, spiritual guides model for our clients healthy and balanced living. Make sure you live a life that is inspiring to your clients.

Have relationships outside of work. It is dangerous for a spiritual guide to live in a bubble where their only significant relationships are their clients. The *Code of Ethics* puts it best: "It is by having friendship and intimacy needs met outside of spiritual direction relationships that [directors] are best able to assure their directees of objectivity and freedom from any of their own hidden (and usually unconscious) emotional agendas."[4]

Never discriminate. While it is, of course, the right of the spiritual guide to choose with whom they work, it is never appropriate to discriminate on the basis of race, religion, age, gender or gender identity, sexual orientation, economic status, physical ability, marital status, political stances, national origin or ethnicity. Directors may turn clients away for reasons other than discrimination. For example, a female director may choose to only work with women because she feels most adequate and equipped for that client base. When turning someone away, always offer a suitable referral.

Maintain a list of other professionals for referrals. In the event that the spiritual guide has reached a limit to what he or she can do for a client, or if it becomes clear the client needs some other or additional help, be ready to refer them to someone you know and trust. In particular, spiritual directors should know a few mental health counselors and spiritual directors they can feel confident referring people to.

Periodically check in with the client for evaluation. The guidance relationship needs to work for the client. Brief check-ins every few months at the end of a session are appropriate. It can be as simple as a question of "how has your spiritual life changed over the time we have been working together?"

End the relationship with kindness. If the spiritual guide must initiate the ending of the relationship, it is important to do so gently and, if possible, with a closing ritual. When the directee terminates, they do so in whatever manner they choose. Although it may be difficult, the spiritual director must graciously accept the termination and never try to talk a client out of leaving. Once a directee has ended a relationship—even if they do it by cancelling and not rescheduling another appointment, the director should not contact the directee about the action. We don't want to chase after our clients or put them in an awkward position by asking for an explanation. Leave the termination in the hands of the Divine.

BASIC RIGHTS OF A SPIRITUAL DIRECTEE

When a person enters a spiritual direction relationship they enter a world in which there is a specific culture and a code of ethics, but no actual oversight body in place to protect their rights.

So, like much else in life, it is a case of "let the buyer beware."

Most spiritual directors are kind, loving and ethical people. But there have been cases of abuse by spiritual directors. So, what can a person expect from a spiritual director?

The client has a right to expect:

To be listened to. This is a basic right and no spiritual guide should violate it. When a person enters direction, it is to share what is on their heart. It is the director's job to listen. When I train directors, I tell them not to interrupt a directee. (Sometimes I get pushback on this!) Directees have a story to tell and even if that story seems twisty, boring or convoluted, if you just give it time you may see the point.

Sessions will be confidential. The material shared with a director should never come back to the client via a third party! Confidentiality also demands that sessions be private (no one popping in to chat with the director either in person or by phone).

To be respected. All beliefs, lifestyles, and choices should be respected by the director. The session is about the client, not the guide.

To be given personal space. Any person seeking spiritual guidance should have their own seat and space to feel comfortable in. The director should never attempt to invade the client's personal space.

To be free to continue or end the relationship according to your needs. Spiritual direction needs to work for the directee. Maybe they need it every three weeks during a difficult period but only need it every two months otherwise. And when it's time to end the relationship, the client has the right to do so without a lot of explanation.

Clean boundaries. Spiritual directors are not to slide into personal friendships with clients. We are not to go into business with them or take on any other significant role in their life. Under no circumstances is it ethical for a spiritual director to have a romantic or sexual relationship with a client. If the spiritual director is violating boundaries, there are some options for the directee. If it feels like a minor breach, then a conversation may clear things up. If it is major and irreparable—such as inappropriate touch or violation of confidentiality—then the relationship should be ended. And if the spiritual guide is connected to a religious organization (for example if they are an ordained person), the directee should contact the institutional body that oversees and regulates the ordination status of the director.

SUPERVISION FOR SPIRITUAL DIRECTORS

Supervision is how spiritual guides grow in understanding of themselves and the Divine. It is the practice of regular meetings with peers or a mentor to discuss (in a confidential manner) situations within direction sessions that seem significant, troubling or puzzling to the director.

Supervision centers on the care, education and growth of the spiritual guide. We bring case studies to supervision to learn about ourselves as directors so that we are free to do the work and so the people we work with get the best of us.

As long as you are offering spiritual direction, you need to be in supervision, whether that is with a peer support group or a trained supervisor to meet with one-on-one.[5] Another option is to find an experienced spiritual guide and request that they serve as a supervisor (explaining to them the nature of the role and what is needed). It is not recommended that you use your own director as supervisor, since that would be a mixing of roles.

In supervision, the spiritual guide writes up a case study, based on the troubling or significant situation, for the supervisor or peer group to work with. Masking the name and any identifying information about the directee, the director will answer some basic questions to help the supervisor understand the context of the situation. In most cases, the director will need to write up a short bit of dialogue from the session that illustrates what was said as well as what was going on inside the director at the time. This write up, called a verbatim, helps supervisors do their work of assisting the director in greater awareness.

The main purpose of supervision is not to figure out how to be a more technically skilled spiritual director (though that may be a by-product). Neither is it a time to analyze what was going on with the directee. Supervision centers on the exploration of the inner feelings and motivations in the director as they participated in the session. It's to create awareness of the motivations and blocks going on inside of us so that we are freer in the future to listen, observe and hold space for our clients.

Supervision is one instance where "it's all about us" so that we can better assist our clients.

There are two excellent books available specifically on the supervision of spiritual directors, and all aspiring or working spiritual directors need to use them as a resource. They are Maureen Conroy's *Looking into the Well: Supervision of Spiritual Directors* and Mary Rose Bumpus and Rebecca Langer's *Supervision of Spiritual Directors: Engaging in Holy Mystery.*[6]

PROJECTION IN SPIRITUAL DIRECTION

Because good spiritual directors do a lot of listening and little personal sharing in a session, we sometimes become a target for other people's projections of anxious thoughts and feelings.

Projection is a term for a defense mechanism people use against their anxiety. A common example of projection is a situation when I am angry at the actions of another person, but instead of accepting my anger, I accuse the other person of being angry. It's a way to distance ourselves from our disturbing inner thoughts by experiencing them *as if the thoughts and feelings belong to the other person.*

The person who is being projected onto (for the purposes of our discussion, the spiritual director) may end up feeling agitated, surprised, angry or otherwise uneasy. It's no fun to be the receiving end of other people's anxiety.

However—and this is really important for spiritual guides to understand—if we are able to calmly receive this projected material, we may help the client grow to a point where they are able to accept their troubling thoughts and feelings. If spiritual directors are not able to "roll with it," so to speak, the directee may withdraw, missing an opportunity for growth.

Psychologist Dr. Rich Muszynski has a few tips for anyone working with projection:[7]

- *Understand that it's not about you.* Projection is not personal (even if the one doing the projecting insists that it is). Bracket or set aside your own unease about the situation until you have time alone to process it.
- *Be a container for the client.* Think of yourself offering an imaginary container that can hold all the anxiety the person is trying to give to you. Lovingly accept where they are and what they are (metaphorically) putting into the bucket. The job of the spiritual director is to pull some items out of the bucket and explore with the directee how these feelings are affecting their spirit.
- *Never get defensive.* If you are caught off guard as someone is depositing their anxiety into your container, simply ask them to tell you more about what they are feeling. Keep the emphasis on them and not on you.
- *Be curious about what is going on.* It may be difficult at first, but the best attitude you can take when being projected onto is curiosity. Know that with practice you will get better at being that loving container.
- *Don't accept abuse.* Offering a loving container does not mean being a doormat or an emotional punching bag. If calm, graceful curiosity and deep listening skills don't seem to work and the directee is becoming aggressive or dangerous, the director has the right to draw the conversation to a close and find safety (such situations in spiritual direction are rare).

Being the container for another person's anxiety is hard work and requires some peaceful reflection time after a session. This is where supervision is crucial, because if we aren't careful we could find that we project our own anxiety onto others. In supervision we gain the proper awareness, so that we can acknowledge and own the full range of our feelings and thoughts.

TRANSFERENCE AND COUNTERTRANSFERENCE IN SPIRITUAL DIRECTION

Spiritual directors encounter some of the same psychological dynamics as therapists, teachers, pastors and others in helping professions. The most common are transference and counter-transference, two ways humans project our unconscious feelings onto another person.

TRANSFERENCE is the natural, to-be-expected process by which a person seeking help transfers their own feelings, thoughts, impulses and fantasies about a person from their past (feelings not fully resolved) to the helper (in our case, the spiritual director). The directee is not aware of this transference of feelings. An example of this might be a directee who reacts negatively to a director who happens to look a little like the father who punished them harshly as a child.

COUNTERTRANSFERENCE is similar. It refers to the process by which the person providing help—in this case the spiritual director—reacts to his or her own feelings, thoughts, impulses and fantasies aroused by the directee. An example of this might be a director becoming overly protective of a young directee who reminds them of their son or daughter. The director's task when confronted with countertransference is to discern and differentiate which emotional reactions are coming from their own past and which may be coming from the transference of the person seeking help.

All this may seem complicated and daunting, but the good news is that both dynamics are relatively easy to work with, provided the spiritual guide has a trained supervisor to work with. Many times, a supervisor is the first person to *notice* that transference or countertransference has occurred within a direction relationship. This is why it is so important for spiritual directors to write up and discuss all situations that bring up heightened emotions, especially situations that make them feel uneasy, confused, angry or sad.

Transference and countertransference are opportunities for personal growth both for the director and the directee. Spiritual directors should always be curious about what is going on in the relationship between them and the directee. If transference is suspected, the director can then give voice to that curiosity and explore it with the client, using simple prompts such as "tell me more about this." Bringing unspoken dynamics to the light fosters inner growth, especially as the spiritual guide remains calm and treats the dynamics as normal. After moving through transference or countertransference, a stronger direction relationship is possible.

One caution, though. If the spiritual guide is not careful about boundaries and allows transference or counter-transference to move the relationship into a re-enactment of a relationship from the past, the relationship will be destroyed and the opportunity for growth truncated. This is especially true with a romantic or intimate relationship between director and directee—a destructive and highly unethical situation.

CONCLUSION

Newly trained spiritual directors usually find ethical principles daunting, especially since there are considerable gray areas. While some boundaries are fixed (no sexual relationships, no violating confidentiality) most are somewhat flexible, and spiritual directors, like other helping professionals, will learn where their boundaries need to be from trial and error. The *Code of Ethics for Spiritual Directors* puts it best: "The binding force behind this code comes not from words on paper, but from each spiritual director's ever-developing relationship with God. No one of us may live up to all that is written here—but, if we err, let it be on the side of love."[8]

NOTES

1. *A Code of Ethics for Spiritual Directors,* Dove Publications 1992.
2. Found online at http://www.sdiworld.org/publications/guidelines-ethical-conduct
3. *A Code of Ethics for Spiritual Directors,* Dove Publications 1992, p. 9.
4. *A Code of Ethics for Spiritual Directors,* Dove Publications 1992, p. 4.
5. Individual supervision usually costs about the same price as a spiritual direction session. You can find trained supervisors on Spiritual Directors International's "Seek and Find Guide."
6. These books are listed in *Works Cited* at the end of the book.
7. Gratitude to Dr. Rich Muszynski, a former faculty member of the Hesychia School of Spiritual Direction for his many lectures on projection, transference and counter-transference from which this section draws.
8. *A Code of Ethics for Spiritual Directors,* Dove Publications 1992, p. 16.

10

TRAINING OF SPIRITUAL DIRECTORS

The Spirit blows where it will, making spiritual guidance impossible to standardize.[1]

In a practical sense, anyone can hang a shingle and start offering spiritual direction. But that's a really bad idea, because if you don't have some training—either by apprenticing or attending a formation and training program—you can be at best, incompetent, and at worst, harmful.

Having the word direction or guide in our title implies to some that we actively move people along a particular path, giving advice and pulling the reins in here and there. *But as I've pointed out many times in this book, we are not that kind of guide. We are not gurus.* And people who are not adequately trained in the art of spiritual direction may slide into guru mode, thinking they are doing God's work, when in fact all they are doing is satisfying some needy place within themselves.

By far the most ethical and sound way to become a spiritual director is to make the commitment to attend and graduate from a program that trains people in the art.

WHAT BRINGS PEOPLE TO TRAINING

Most spiritual directors come to training in one of three ways:

1. *People seek them out.* They notice that as they draw closer to the Divine, people in their life come to them for a listening ear. Many say, "I was already doing this for people so I figured I'd get trained so I can do it properly."
2. *Desire to give back.* They have received so many blessings from being in spiritual direction that they want to offer that blessing to others. (This was my path.)
3. *Their vocation would be enhanced by training.* A job they have requires them to work in a capacity of spiritual guide and they want to be more effective at it. (This would include clergy, religious educators, chaplains, therapists, health care workers and social workers.)

Some people may look at that list and wonder why it doesn't include "I was called by God to be a spiritual director." That's because "call" is a slippery concept for many people. It can mean so many different things. I prefer to have people look at their desires and motivations clearly and determine later if they are called. I also believe—after a decade or more of running a spiritual direction training program—that even if people don't feel called to be a spiritual director after attending, the training will make them more spiritually aware human beings in their interactions with just about everyone.

The bottom line is, you can be trained without being called, but if you are called, *you really need to get trained.*

HOW TO FIND A TRAINING PROGRAM

There are programs to fit everyone's desire and need for training.

The best place to start your search for a program is SDI's website.[2] There are now hundreds of education, formation and training (EFT) programs for spiritual directors listed on SDI's web page about EFT.[3]

The next step would be to talk with any and all spiritual directors you know and ask them where they got their training and how they feel about the education they received. Calling retreat centers is usually helpful as well. Ask them where they find their spiritual directors and what training programs they recommend.

If you are searching for a "best of" list you will be disappointed. SDI doesn't rank programs and it can be difficult to compare programs. Each has its own emphasis and flavor. You just have to do your homework.

A few programs have been around a long time and are well known. They include:

- The Shalem Institute for Spiritual Formation in Washington, DC
- The Program in Spiritual Direction Formation at the Mercy Center in Burlingame, CA
- The Dominican Center for Religious Development in Cambridge, MA
- Upper Room Ministries Living Prayer Center in Nashville
- The Chaplaincy Institute's Interfaith Spiritual Direction Certificate Program in Berkeley, CA
- The Hesychia School of Spiritual Direction in Tucson, AZ
- The Center for Spirituality and Justice at Fordham University, Bronx, NY
- The Institute for Spiritual Leadership in Chicago

- The Diploma in the Art of Spiritual Direction at San Francisco Theological Seminary
- Biola University Institute for Spiritual Formation

Every year new programs emerge. Some are academic and based at a seminary or institution of higher education, some at retreat centers, and others are independent.

FORMATS OF TRAINING PROGRAMS

Some people choose a program based on a format that best suits them. A few to consider are:

1. *Residential.* You and your cohort stay on the grounds of a retreat center or some pre-arranged housing facility and attend classes together. Residential programs bring people from all over the world to study together, usually in an accelerated and condensed period of time. Some residential programs involve only one gathering and others require that you return for study over a period of time. Residential programs may or may not require that participants do an internship period in which they take on clients and visit supervisors for additional training. The greatest value to a residential program tends to be the relationships made by studying with a close-knit cohort.

2. *Regional.* These programs hold learning sessions on a regular basis—monthly on a Saturday over a two-year period is common. A regional program is ideal for a person who has one nearby and is not able or willing to take several weeks off in a year for training.

3. *Hybrids.* These training programs combine face-to-face gatherings with online or distance learning in order to save travel time, and in some cases, money.

4. *Online.* Everything seems to be going online these days, and while I am not familiar at this time with spiritual direction training programs that are completely online, I'm sure a few can be found. The downside to a purely online program would be the lack of in-person interactions as you learn.

5. *Apprenticing.* For centuries, this was the training spiritual guides received, usually within their religious orders. Trainees would learn from someone who had been offering spiritual direction for many years and then start doing it when the mentor felt they were ready. This model may still be in operation; however, I am not familiar with anyone offering their services as an official mentor-trainer. A potential downside to this model is that the apprentice only has one teacher, and the certificate of completion would be backed up by the word of only one person.

WHAT TO LOOK FOR IN A TRAINING PROGRAM

Finding the right program is a discernment process, taking time, prayer and attention.

What should you be looking for? While most spiritual direction training programs teach a method that is more evocative than directive, they don't all teach it in the same way. Here are some key elements to look for:

- *A program that stresses the contemplative nature of spiritual direction.* If it's not rooted in a contemplative tradition that honors silence, waiting and gentle exploration, then it could be a program that has a particular agenda (Evangelism? Discipleship? Coaching?). That wouldn't make it a bad program, but those practices are different from spiritual direction. Delve deep into what the program is really about before you make a commitment.

- *A program that includes a fair amount of practical experience doing spiritual direction.* You want to learn the art of spiritual direction by doing it under the watchful eye of a teacher or supervisor. It does little good for programs to send participants off in pairs to do spiritual direction with one another with no one around to watch what is going on. Look for programs that have strong supervised practicums that allow each participant to serve as a spiritual director in a real session (not role playing) with a teacher or other members of the small group viewing the session. Debriefing what happened in the session is hard work but essential, and good teachers know how to give gentle and helpful observations. If you only do spiritual direction with your peers, without a teacher supervising, it's likely you haven't been told the full truth about how you came across as a spiritual director. You need that information before you strike out on your own and start taking directees.

- *A program that is likely to be around for a few years.* Sadly, many programs just don't make it even though their structure is such that it takes two years or more to get a certificate of completion. It is frustrating to start one program and then have to start another one because your first choice went under financially. Investigate the history of the program you are interested in. Talk to the director of the program and find out if they have a refund option in the event of cancellation. Have they ever cancelled a program? Talk to graduates as well. The training program you choose should be a resource for you even after you graduate.

- *A program that fits your personality.* If you want a

147

program that stresses Ignatian spirituality then don't go to a Zen retreat house; find one rooted in Ignatian spiritual exercises. If desert spirituality is what calls to you, then find a program based in a desert. To find what fits for you, make a lot of phone calls to directors of programs. Tell them a bit about yourself and ask questions about any aspect of formation that concerns you.

- *A program that fits your life.* As mentioned before, there are many formats for training. After you make a short list of programs you are interested in, consider which ones on that list are the most practical for you. Some are more expensive than others. Some require more time off from work. Since there are quite a few programs out there now, there should be one that ticks off all the boxes you have on your wish list.

CONCLUSION

Although I have written a lot here about training programs for spiritual directors, and although I have warned about the danger of practicing spiritual guidance without training, it is important to note that not all spiritual directors have been through training. You may find an excellent spiritual director who has been working for years but never went to Shalem, Mercy Center, Hesychia School or anywhere else. This may especially be true if you are outside the U.S. or Europe.

Years ago, before the explosion of training and formation programs, spiritual directors learned the art from another spiritual director, and they relied heavily on their God-given gift for listening and asking the right questions. So, some of our oldest and best spiritual directors learned "on the job."

Historically, spiritual direction was, and still is, something a person either has natural gifts for or develops the skills to do. It is possible to find the world's best spiritual director simply by looking for a person who has the qualities of unconditional love and acceptance and who is able to listen, help you explore, and encourage you in discernment.

Additionally, training doesn't guarantee that a person will work out well for you as a spiritual guide. In the Western world, we are certification crazy. We want certificates and we look for them in our service providers. But since there is no *standard* certification for spiritual directors, there is no standard to which all spiritual directors can be held. We in the spiritual direction community are not even sure we want educational standards because there are so many different philosophies about spiritual direction.

Having said all that, I do look for trained directors when I seek one for myself and when I look for teachers in the training program I administer. Combine a deep connection to the Divine with a few natural gifts and good training and you have a spiritual guide you can trust.

NOTES

1. That is not the case, however, in some jurisdictions for people offering psychic, intuitive or medium readings. In Tucson, AZ, psychics must register with the city! Not sure who oversees this fortune-telling marketplace, but there is a fee and a license involved.
2. www.sdiworld.org
3. www.sdiworld.org/eft

SETTING UP YOUR SPIRITUAL DIRECTION PRACTICE

Once you have received training in the art of spiritual guidance and want to get started doing it, you have a lot of practical matters to consider.

WHAT KIND OF SPIRITUAL DIRECTOR WILL YOU BE?

There are many ways to be a spiritual director.

Some hang out a shingle and set up private practices in order to meet with people one-on-one. These directors hope to see quite a few people each month—something on the order of 20 or more.

Others do this ministry as a side endeavor to complement other work they do—and they may only accept two or three directees a month. Many clergy or full-time workers in another profession fit into this category.

There are also those who don't see individual clients but seek to transform their current jobs by approaching them "with the eyes of a spiritual director." Again, many clergy don't have time to take on directees but find that spiritual direction skills help them rethink and revise the way they do pastoral care with congregants.

Some spiritual directors prefer to only do group direction. A small but growing number offer their gifts to organizations, doing a kind of corporate spiritual direction.

You will want to spend time with these three questions:

1. *What are my particular gifts as a spiritual guide?* Reflecting on your gifts and making a list of them helps you discern what your practice will look like. It also helps build confidence.
2. *What is my desire for doing spiritual direction?* Consider your deepest and truest desires in life and how they are leading you as a spiritual guide.
3. *What is the world's need for the kind of spiritual guidance I offer?* Practically speaking, you need to know if there is a market for your particular gifts as a spiritual director. You can find this out through research, the response to your marketing and your own wisdom after taking on a few clients.

The answer lies in the "sweet spot" where those three answers intersect.

Let me give you an example. When I first started out as a spiritual director, I had a deep desire to work with church bodies in discernment, and I felt (hoped!) I had gifts for that work. I traveled around offering my services to churches, meeting with boards and pastors. I had very few takers. At that time in my life and the life of these churches, there was no perceived need for what I was selling. So, it was not my sweet spot, at least not at that time. However, individuals came out of the woodwork looking for spiritual direction with an emphasis on discernment. I accepted that as my sweet spot and found my way into private practice.

Sadly, some people have the desire to do one-on-one guidance in private practice, but find they don't attract clients or have the gifts for it. Maybe they do, however, have gifts for group work. The Spirit has a way of working all this out in us.

The discernment around what kind of spiritual director you are called to be never ends. While I didn't get to do the kind of corporate discernment work with churches that I wanted to years ago, I do occasionally get the opportunity to do the work now—some 15 years later. After a few years of continued marketing around the practice of discernment, I was offered a contract to do group spiritual direction and discernment with a church-sponsored mission volunteer group—a job that lasted 10 years. And I am delighted to bring these skills to other aspects of my career, such as assisting the Hesychia School of Spiritual Direction's Leadership Team in discerning where God is leading us as a school.

Be creative and persistent, because you never know where your training will lead. Sweet spots abound.

FINDING THE RIGHT SPACE

Spiritual directors must pay special attention to the physical space they use for sessions. It must be:

1. Relatively quiet.
2. Private. No interruptions.
3. Comfortable.

You'll want the space to mirror the contemplative work done in it. The best spaces are artistically beautiful, yet not overtly religious.

You may be wondering, "What's wrong with putting my religious knick-knacks around the room?" Well, what is religiously significant to you may be a huge distraction to your client. Directors don't have to go overboard and have a blank room, but think carefully about the art you use in the space. It should not be a distraction.

For instance, I was once invited for centering prayer into a spiritual direction room (in a church) that had words and phrases pasted tastefully around the room. Things like "Believe" and "Faith." That didn't bother me. But the candle in the center of the room had the words from a Sunday school song I used to know as a child: *Your word is a lamp unto my feet and a light unto my path.* As I sat and tried to become contemplative, that little ditty kept going through my mind as a constant distraction. After that I became vigilant about how my own spiritual direction room needed to look and feel!

At Home or Away?

Many spiritual directors use a room in their home for this work. If that feels right for you, then go for it. Just be aware of drawbacks to using your home. Someone else living there may feel constrained by having to be quiet or avoid the room you are using. Pets can be a huge distraction. Also, think carefully about how comfortable you are having people in your home. Some people love to entertain and keep their house in sparkling condition all the time for that purpose. Others (like me) find it a bit anxiety-producing to run around to pick up my significant other's socks and chase dust bunnies down before every appointment. Know your comfort level with using your own home.

Rented Rooms

Many spiritual guides, especially those who are accepting a large number of clients, rent a space they can control. This is costly, but I have found it much more conducive to a contemplative experience. I have rented a small room in an office of therapists. It cost me about the price of seeing five directees a month. Since I usually see about 20 a month, I find this to be an acceptable cost of doing business. If renting commercial space seems out of the question, see if a church or non-profit agency near you would offer you free or low-cost space.

Donated Space

When you use donated space, you get a bargain, but you have less control over what the space looks and feels like. I have worked in church rooms with a lot of religious posters on the wall, which did not feel contemplative to me. Also, church offices can be noisy and lacking in privacy.

When using a donated space, it is customary to offer something of value in return. I currently see people in an office at my church, and in exchange for being able to use that space, I give the lead pastor four vouchers a month to hand out to people who want to try spiritual direction.

Finding the right space for spiritual direction is a challenge. You may have to try a few different spaces out before you find your "promised land" in spiritual direction.

Using Technology

Some spiritual guides don't have to worry about paying for a space because they use technology so well. When you market yourself online, you will likely get inquiries from people who don't live near you. If you are willing and are comfortable with technology, you may want to consider:

Working by phone. Almost everyone now has a phone in their pocket or bag, and if you are willing to do spiritual direction by phone you have a whole world of potential clients. I know a spiritual director who works mostly by phone and has sessions sitting in his car if he needs privacy while away from home. When working by phone with people far away from you, don't forget to factor in time zone differences.

A drawback to working by phone is that, as we all know, technology is not perfect. Calls get dropped, sound quality can be bad and background noise can be a distraction. Before you work by phone, figure out what you will do in each case, because you will face these situations. I let clients know that if the call is dropped, I will call them right back. If sound quality is an issue, try redialing or moving to a better location. (When working from home I use a landline for better quality on my end.) There should be little to no background noise on your end—make sure of that—but if the client is in a noisy place you'll need to ask them to move. It's impossible to listen carefully to someone if you can't hear them.

Working by online video. Computer software that enables live video conversation is being used now by most people who have computers, tablets and smartphones. It's a wonderful tool for working at a distance—if you are comfortable with the technology. You may even choose to work online with people in your metro area, especially if they work far from your office and find the commute difficult to manage. Programs like Skype, Zoom, FaceTime and Google Hangouts are all used by spiritual directors around the world. Just as with phones, you must be ready for glitches in live online conversation. Sessions can easily get dropped or the video can freeze at any time.

Just like meeting someone in person, you will want to make a good impression online. Arrange a pleasant backdrop for yourself, play around with lighting to figure out what looks good, and always check out your audio and video settings prior to the session. If using a laptop, tablet or smartphone, have it secured in front of you so the picture doesn't jiggle around on your client. Also, make sure the microphone on your device is not obstructed, so that you can be heard. I like to use a headset (microphone and earphone) that plugs into my computer for the best sound quality.

However, some people don't want to look like a telemarketer while in session!

Work by email or chat. While I haven't tried this, there are a few spiritual directors I know who work with clients who prefer email interactions. There are different ways to do this, so you would need to work out with your client what works best for both of you. Generally, they pay you monthly and then you would share back and forth by email according to your agreement. Some spiritual guides allow a set number of email letters each month and they ask clients to read and write their letters prayerfully.

I haven't tried it, but a session could take place in real time with director and directee writing back and forth on a program that offers the chat or direct messaging function.

SETTING YOUR FEE

Spiritual directors are no different from anyone else: we need to make a living. Like all freelancers, we have to figure out what we are going to charge for our service. There is no standard fee or even agreed-upon scale for spiritual directors. There are lots of ways spiritual directors approach this.

- *Find out the going rate for your region.* Ask around and find out what most directors in your area charge for a session. Your rate should be comparable. You can try pricing yourself higher and see if the market can handle it. Or you can go lower and do "value pricing." If you are leaning toward the latter, think carefully about the overall effect on other spiritual directors if you give yourself away for free or for low, low cost. In Phoenix, AZ, where I live, the going rate for spiritual direction is between $50 to $80 a session. In Los Angeles and San Francisco, spiritual directors are charging $100 or more per hour. In rural areas, where the cost of living is low, a session might cost $40. One way to gauge is to find out how much fitness trainers or massage therapists in your area are charging per hour and ask for a similar amount. Others consider how much time and money they spent in training and come up with a price they feel is justified.

- *Working with a range.* You may want to request a range that allows the directee to choose what they pay you (within reason). A friend of mine charges $50 to $75 per session and says most of the people he sees with full-time jobs pay him the high end. This approach does put some pressure on the directee to decide if he or she will pay you the minimum or the maximum. If you are the kind of person who will feel slighted if your directee chooses to pay you the minimum, then don't take this approach!

- *Rate based on client's income.* Some directors ask directees to pay them whatever *the directee's* hourly wage rate is. If that makes you feel better about taking their money, go for it. Keep in mind, though, you are only seeing them for one hour a month. So, although it seems totally fair (an hour of my time is worth the same as an hour of yours), this will probably not work in your favor unless you live in a high wage region of the country. Very few people in Arizona make $60 per hour, yet my directees pay that for a session with me because it's only once a month.

If you are not comfortable asking for money in exchange for your time as a spiritual director, I encourage you to examine that resistance. Every now and then I hear about a spiritual guide doing this work for free, mostly because they don't think it's right to make a spiritual practice transactional. While that may feel like the right thing to do, it makes it that much harder for those of us who do this for a living to get by.

Try working through the discomfort and ask for what you are worth. (Your training wasn't free, was it?) After you do this a few times, you will see that most people appreciate spiritual direction and want to pay you. You will feel more powerful and you will be making money doing something meaningful and valuable that you love.

Pro Bono Work

I believe in charging, but I also feel strongly that spiritual direction is not just for the comfortably well-off. I do a few *pro bono* or free sessions each year for people who are unemployed, on disability, or on a very low or fixed income. Sliding scales are also offered. If someone balks at my going rate, I usually ask them, "What are you able to pay?" and then accept that rate from them.

TRACKING INCOME

While we're on the topic of money, a few more guidelines to mention:

- *Records.* Keep good track of your spiritual direction income. Make sure your records are kept confidential as well.
- *Taxes.* You will be paying taxes on the income. We don't need spiritual directors taking money under the table and getting busted by the IRS. It's unethical, illegal and creates bad press. As a self-employed person, you will be paying estimated taxes four times a year just like every other freelancer in the world.
- *Trades.* Don't offer your services as a trade for in-kind services. I also do not recommend taking gifts (barter)

in exchange for spiritual direction, although I know some religious orders do that. Trade or barter makes bookkeeping for tax purposes difficult.

- *How to collect.* Have directees pay you at the end of the session. Cash, check, or online (using PayPal, Venmo, or other apps, including the various gadgets you can get from money management websites) are all fine with me. Sometimes people forget to bring their checks or cash and then I ask them to mail it in. If you work with people by phone, set a deadline for the money to come in. You may also send an invoice after every session if that works for you. I invoice clients right after a session unless they have already paid me.

MARKETING A SPIRITUAL DIRECTION PRACTICE

How is it possible that spiritual direction has been around for ages, yet so few people know about it?

Spiritual direction should not be a secret. It's time for spiritual directors to gather resources and share the news about this practice with the world.

However, discussing the marketing of spiritual direction can be a touchy subject. There are some spiritual directors who reject the idea of advertising their availability. In fact, *A Code of Ethics for Spiritual Directors* (Dove Publications), states:

> Traditionally, spiritual directors have not publicized or advertised their services, or promoted themselves in other ways.[1]

That was published in 1992, long before people began using the Internet as a communication tool. Today if a spiritual director is available and wants it known they are offering spiritual direction, it is *expected* they will use social media, websites and email marketing, as well as the traditional business cards and brochures to get the word out.

The Soft Sell

For spiritual entrepreneurs, soft marketing is better than the hard sell. Much like the organization Alcoholics Anonymous, we tend to rely on attraction rather than promotion. Soft marketing involves describing your service, educating the public about it and then waiting for clients to come to you instead of recruiting people as clients.

As you prepare your marketing materials, make sure your information sticks to basic facts and is devoid of any claims or promises about spiritual direction.[2] Never promise a specific outcome, such as an end to grief or the healing of a spiritual wound. We may hope for spiritual growth on the part of the client, but we do not guarantee it.

Referrals and Networking

The word-of-mouth referral has been around since the time of the desert monastics. It is the most common way to receive directees. Which means a spiritual director usually begins with one or two clients who then promote the practice to friends and colleagues. This is the slowest form of marketing, but it is effective.

Once you become a spiritual director, let all your friends and colleagues know and tell them you are accepting clients.

Lots of people in helping professions may also want to send you referrals: physicians, nurses, psychologists, religious leaders, pastors, denominational leaders, chaplains, campus ministers, retreat center directors and social workers. These professionals meet with people daily who may be in need of spiritual direction. Give them your printed material, such as business cards, brochures or website addresses, so they have them on hand to make a referral.

Network with other spiritual directors as well. Join Spiritual Directors International (SDI) and get on a list of directors in your region.[3] There may even be an association of local spiritual directors you can join.

Because many spiritual guides are naturally introverts, networking can be intimidating. I recommend the method that Bob Burg promotes in his book *Endless Referrals*.[4] Instead of going to an event and handing out business cards to people you don't know, Burg suggests you attend events and do the following:

1. *Engage* someone new by being curious and interested in who they are and what brings them to the event. Ask them about their family, occupation, what they do for fun, or what is important to them. You don't need to talk about yourself or your occupation at first.
2. *Think about how you might be able to help them in their work.* For example, I sometimes ask clergy when I first meet them, "How might I know someone I'm talking with would be a good fit for your congregation?" (Note: I am *not* saying that I will, in spiritual direction, steer people to their church. I am implying that if I work with someone who might be a good fit and they ask for the name of a church to visit, I might suggest their church.)
3. *Ask for their business card.* They will be delighted to give you their card and by this time in the conversation, the person has probably warmed up to you enough to ask you what you do. Have a good, short "elevator speech" about spiritual direction ready and then give them your card.
4. *After the event, send the person a note following up on the conversation.* Something simple, like, "It was nice to meet

you and hope your business (or whatever) keeps
growing and improving."

Websites

Online marketing is here to stay and it is the second-best way
(after word of mouth) to market spiritual direction. Websites are
safe places for seekers to go and read about the kind of spiritual
direction or guidance being offered. It's an educational tool to let
the world know what spiritual direction is and how it is different
from other forms of guidance, such as therapy, life coaching or
intuition counseling.

Depending on one's ease with technology, websites can be
simple to create using click-and-build programs offered by a web
hosting service. If you feel intimidated by the prospect of building
your own website, there are lots of companies that will build one
for you—for a price.

Your website may be the traditional one with a home page and
then several other pages for more information. Or you may
choose to create a solo sales page, sometimes called a landing
page.

It is helpful to employ a consultant (or grab a millennial from
your family) to find out how to make your website search-engine-
friendly. Search engine optimization (SEO) techniques change
constantly, but the best rule of thumb is to fill your website with
dependable, engaging content and update it frequently (blogs are
good for that). Trying to keep up with SEO algorithm changes is
not a meaningful contemplative activity for most spiritual
directors!

Blogs

If you enjoy writing, blogs are an excellent way to reach out to seekers. In fact, this very book began its life as a blog (Spiritual Direction 101 for Patheos).[5]

Your blog could reside with an aggregate that publishes many blogs, such as Patheos or Huffington Post, or it can be a page on your website, which is the easiest to set up and control. Many spiritual guides and directors use personal essays based on their own spiritual paths for their blog posts. There's a whole culture and lots of advice about blogging for the greatest reach, so don't get overwhelmed by all the "dos" and "don'ts." Just make sure your friends know about your blog and have them spread the word.

One caution: It can be tempting to share content from specific spiritual direction sessions in a blog, but remember the ethic of confidentiality. Make sure what you share is from your own life, not from the lives of your clients.

If you are interested in blogging but are not sure how to start, why not be a guest-blogger who contributes to an existing blog? To locate these, do an online search for "blogs on spiritual direction" and you will find a rich feast. Once you find one in particular that you like, contact the blogger and ask if they ever use guest bloggers. You may be surprised at how easy it is to find bloggers willing to help.

Social Media

Facebook, Twitter, Instagram, LinkedIn, Pinterest and Snapchat are a few of the most popular social networking sites online. These are ways to interact with people you know, and also strangers, depending on how you determine your privacy settings. Facebook is by far (at this writing) the most popular for sharing content, with Instagram close behind (its focus being photos with commentary). Twitter is a micro-blogging platform in which you send short messages to those who have chosen to follow you. Facebook, Twitter and LinkedIn are all popular venues for sharing articles and blog posts of interest to spiritual seekers.

Probably the social networks most used by spiritual directors are Facebook and LinkedIn. Facebook is now used by about 75% of people in the world, so you can see why anyone would want to use it in marketing. In the spiritual marketplace, Facebook pages are commonly used in addition to a website—some use it instead of a website—and can be set up for individual use or as a professional page. It's a place to post your thoughts for the day, inspirational photos, memes you have created (photos with words overlaid to make a point), articles you like or promos for upcoming events. LinkedIn is for professional contacts and has a more serious feel to it than Facebook, but it operates mostly the same way.

For people who have not spent much time with social media, there is a learning curve. So, if you want to use it but aren't sure how, check out online tutorials or ask a friend who is familiar with the social networks you want to use to help you figure them out.

Once you are on social media, the care and feeding of your pages is essential. Update them on a regular basis. Don't just lurk and read other people's material, but have some fun—engage with people who are interesting to you. Reply to those who comment. You can expand your circle of spiritual entrepreneurs by showing up and sharing on social media.

For those of us who use social media a lot (yes, me!), a warning: It's easy to waste time online. It is mind-blowing what you can find on social media. But introverts especially are susceptible to falling down rabbit holes following links and tweets and Facebook articles. If you want to stay updated on your pages, but don't want to become addicted to social media, check them only a couple of times a day and you won't miss much.

Email

Email seems old-fashioned to some but it's still a great marketing tool. Sales gurus swear by the email newsletter—a free, content-rich publication sent on a regular basis to the inboxes of people who have signed up for it. People like these newsletters because they don't have to remember to go to a particular website to fetch their news—it just comes to their box and they can take their time getting to it. Plus, if they like it, they will forward it to friends and you quickly get new subscribers. If you want to start a newsletter, check out some of the free or inexpensive do-it-yourself email marketing platforms such as MailChimp or Constant Contact.

Published Material

You may also want to go old-school and promote yourself in print media.

Articles. Publishing pieces in newspapers, magazines and newsletters about spiritual direction or spiritual practices can be effective. Local newspapers frequently carry articles about spiritual direction or events of a spiritual nature. *Presence,* a peer-reviewed journal from Spiritual Directors International, seeks articles, essays, poems and book reviews about spiritual guidance.

Brochures. The golden oldy of marketing! It's great to have paper goods to hand out in networking situations. I think of the brochure as the "website on paper" because it should give the reader the information they need to know in order to get excited about spiritual direction and contact you—just like your website.

Some guidelines for creating a nice-looking brochure:

1. *Explain spiritual direction,* your qualifications and give contact information. Give the essentials, such as your bio and your basic philosophy of spiritual guidance, but don't load your brochure up with too much information. Keep the look contemplative, like the

practice. If you are charging a fee, be sure to put the amount in the brochures. It's one of the first items of interest people look for.

2. *Take advantage of easy brochure-builders.* Use a software program designed to create brochures. Microsoft Publisher is a well-known computer program, but you can find brochure-builders online with Canva, Befunky or on the website of a publisher such as VistaPrint.

3. *Beware of abusing copyright laws.* Use only art that is not copyrighted and photos that you took or ones that are clearly in the creative commons and available for free use.

Business cards are another long-standing marketing tool. Professionals always carry cards with them to share with people who show an interest in their work. Your cards don't have to be fancy. One spiritual director I know simply has his name, the title "Spiritual Director" and his phone number. Works just fine. I include a bit more—such as my website address and a tag line about spiritual direction.

Cards may be designed on your computer, in a publishing program or on the websites of many printers. VistaPrint is well known for offering free, colorful and interesting backgrounds to choose from. Staples and other local printers can also help you create your calling cards.

If you're not sure what you want in a card you can always create one with a publishing software program and print them out on your printer at home using pre-cut sheets of business cards available at office supply stores. That way you can play around, creating ten or twenty instead of hundreds at a time.

Flyers. For special events you are hosting or need to promote, you may want to create a one-page flyer to hand out. Like your brochure, it should include the essentials, such as bio, contact information and price.

Public Speaking

An essential part of the educational marketing of spiritual direction involves practitioners getting out in public and talking about it! Teach, preach, present workshops or seminars, lead or work at retreats, and talk to local community groups. Any place you go to talk about spirituality is a place where you should describe spiritual direction and distribute your cards and brochures.

Webinars are popular ways to teach people about spiritual direction. Spiritual Directors International leads the way with affordable, low-tech webinars on subjects of interest within the spiritual guidance community. Creating a webinar takes some dedication, research and technical familiarity, but it can be a source of income as well as a way of allowing potential new clients to warm up to you.

More Marketing Ideas

- Post flyers in coffeehouses, libraries, non-profits, wellness centers, assisted living facilities, hospices.
- Visit wellness centers, counseling offices and stores that carry spiritual books and materials and introduce yourself.
- Find a related job to use as a platform for talking about spiritual direction: religious educator, retreat leader or helper, chaplain or hospice worker.
- Create a direct mail campaign targeted to organizations in need of your services. (That's right, snail mail is still around!)

MARKETING MISTAKES—WHAT NOT TO DO

Please do *not* call yourself a

- *Professional* Spiritual Director
- *Certified* Spiritual Director
- *Mentor*
- Any kind of *counselor* or *therapist* (unless you are one in another capacity)

I know it's tempting to call yourself a certified spiritual director, guide or companion. But as has been pointed out a number of times in this book, there is no standard certification process for spiritual directors, so putting the word certified in your title can be misleading. I know people do it all the time—I'm just telling you what SDI would tell you—it's not considered a "best practice."

Don't conjure up fancy titles for yourself that could be deceptive. Yes, there are lots of spiritual directors who do not like the term "director" because of the many connotations of the word "direct." But coming up with a creative term for it that is confusing or misleading is not helpful either. The synonyms I've heard for spiritual direction can be just as problematic as "spiritual director," which is why I prefer the original title. At least a *few* people in the world know what a spiritual director is and the tradition behind what we do. If they don't, your marketing material is the perfect place to give your definition.

If you must create your own term for it, make sure it has integrity. For example, if you call yourself a spiritual counselor (unless you are licensed as a counselor in your state) or a "prayer therapist" you are implying that you counsel, which is not accurate and can get you in trouble with your state licensing boards.

Spiritual director, spiritual guide, or spiritual companion are the most common terms used for the work we do.

NOTES

1. *A Code of Ethics for Spiritual Directors,* p. 15.
2. *Ibid,* p. 16.
3. Once you join SDI you are eligible to be listed in their "Seek and Find Guide."
4. *Endless Referrals: Network Your Everyday Contacts into Sales,* Bob Burg. New York: McGraw-Hill, 2006.
5. Found online at http://www.patheos.com/blogs/spiritualdirection101/

EPILOGUE

How are you feeling about the practice of spiritual direction at this point? I hope you are excited, enthusiastic and feeling empowered to accompany others as they explore their spiritual path.

If, however, you are feeling overwhelmed, take heart. You learn most of this by doing and you will not be perfect at it—ever! That's something we all have in common.

The important thing to remember is *there is grace*. Do your best to follow the principles and guidelines presented in this book, keep going to supervision, take advantage of continuing education, and make use of the many books listed below.

Our world needs more people who are awake, aware and willing to notice where and how the Divine is showing up. That's what spiritual directors do and that's why people come to spiritual direction.

Take good care of yourself.

Stay in touch with the Divine as a way of life.

Share with others this wonderful work you do.

Enjoy the journey.

And if you want to talk more about spiritual direction or just say hello, I invite you to reach out to me at:

teresa@teresablythe.net

PRAYER FOR SPIRITUAL DIRECTORS

Loving Creator,

We offer our hearts, minds, bodies and spirits to you as we seek to be of service to those who come to us for guidance.

May our attention be drawn to places in their story where you are most alive and compelling.

May our words be few and our silence powerful as we make space for our clients to discover their own wisdom.

May we lay aside judgment, bias, assumptions and ego.

May we do no harm.

May we take good care of our hearts, minds, bodies and spirits so we have precious energy to give to this work.

Most of all, may we love, experience, and enjoy you more deeply as a result of this work.

May we be blessed, Holy One.

Amen.

WORKS CITED

Alcoholics Anonymous: Big Book Reference Edition for Addiction Treatment. 2014.

Buckley, Suzanne, ed. *Sacred is the Call: Formation and Transformation in Spiritual Direction Programs.* New York: Crossroad Publishing, 2005.

Bumpus, Mary Rose and Rebecca Bradburn Langer. *Supervision of Spiritual Directors: Engaging in Holy Mystery.* New York: Morehouse Publishing, 2005.

Burg, Bob. *Endless Referrals: Network Your Everyday Contacts into Sales.* New York: McGraw-Hill, 2006.

Burghardt, Walter J. "Contemplation: A long loving look at the Real." *Church* (Winter 1989): 14-18.

Conroy, Maureen, R.S.M. *Looking into the Well: Supervision of Spiritual Directors.* Chicago: Loyola Press, 1995.

Edwards, Tilden. *Living in the Presence: Disciplines for the Spiritual Heart.* San Francisco: HarperCollins, 1987.

Farnham, Suzanne G. and Joseph P. Gill, R. Taylor McLean and Susan Ward. *Listening Hearts: Discerning Call in Community.* New York: Morehouse Publishing, 1991.

Ganss, George E, SJ. *Ignatius of Loyola: The Spiritual Exercises and Selected Works.* New York: Paulist Press, 1991.

Hamm, Thomas D. *Quaker Writings: An Anthology, 1650-1920 (Penguin Classics).* London: Penguin Classics, 2011.

Keller, Catherine. *On the Mystery: Discerning Divinity in Process.* Minneapolis: Fortress Press, 2007.

Leech, Kenneth. *Soul Friend: An Invitation to Spiritual Direction.* San Francisco: HarperCollins, 1980.

Ludwig, Carol. "A Brief History of Spiritual Directors International, Part 1." *Presence.* 8.1 (February 2002).

Ludwig, Carol. "A Brief History of Spiritual Directors International, Part 2." *Presence.* 8.2 (June 2002).

May, Gerald W. *Care of Mind/Care of Spirit: A Psychiatrist Explores Spiritual Direction.* New York: Harper Collins, 1982.

May, Rollo. *Addiction and Grace: Love and Spirituality in the Healing of Addictions.* San Francisco: HarperOne, 2007.

Merton, Thomas. *Spiritual Direction and Meditation.* Collegeville, MN: Liturgical Press, 1960.

Nouwen, Henri (with Michael J. Christensen and Rebecca J. Laird). *Spiritual Direction: Wisdom for the Long Walk of Faith.* New York: HarperCollins, 2006.

Wolff, Pierre. *Discernment: The Art of Choosing Well.* Liguori, MO: Liguori, 1970.

TOPICAL READING LIST

The following is an alphabetical list by topic of books that may be helpful for learning more about specific aspects of spiritual direction and working with people from a variety of backgrounds. This list is not meant to be exhaustive, but merely suggestive of where you might find information you need for the work of spiritual guidance.

SPIRITUAL DIRECTION (GENERAL)

Bakke, Jeannette A. *Holy Invitations: Exploring Spiritual Direction.* Grand Rapids, MI: Baker Books, 2000.

Benner, David. *Sacred Companions: The Gift of Spiritual Friendship and Direction.* Downers Grove, IL: IV Press, 2004.

Edwards, Tilden. *Living in the Presence: Disciplines for the Spiritual Heart.* San Francisco: HarperCollins, 1987.

—. *Spiritual Director, Spiritual Companion: Guide to Tending the Soul.* New York: Paulist Press, 2001.

Gunther, Margaret. *Holy Listening: The Art of Spiritual Direction.* Boston: Cowley Publications, 1992.

Hart, Thomas N. *The Art of Christian Listening.* New York: Paulist Press, 1980.

Leech, Kenneth. *Soul Friend: An Invitation to Spiritual Direction.* San Francisco: HarperCollins, 1980.

Moon, Gary and David Benner, eds. *Spiritual Direction and the Care of Souls: A Guide to Christian Approaches and Practices.* Downers Grove, IL: IV Press, 2004.

Peterson, Eugene H. *The Contemplative Pastor: Returning to the Art of Spiritual Direction.* Grand Rapids, MI: Eerdmans Publishing, 1989.

Phillips, Susan S. *Candlelight: Illuminating the Art of Spiritual Direction (Spiritual Directors International).* New York: Morehouse Publishing, 2008.

Pickering, Sue. *Spiritual Direction: A Practical Introduction.* Norwich: Canterbury Press, 2008.

Ruffing, Janet K. *Spiritual Direction: Beyond the Beginnings.* New York: Paulist Press, 2000.

Smith, Gordon T. *Spiritual Direction: A Guide to Giving and Receiving Direction.* Downers Grove, IL: IV Press, 2014.

Stinissen, Wilfrid. *The Gift of Spiritual Direction: On Spiritual Guidance and Care of the Soul.* Liguori, MO: Liguori Publications, 1999.

HISTORY OF SPIRITUAL DIRECTION

Edwards, Tilden. *Living in the Presence: Disciplines for the Spiritual Heart.* San Francisco: HarperCollins, 1987.

Leech, Kenneth. *Soul Friend: An Invitation to Spiritual Direction.* San Francisco: HarperCollins, 1980.

Ludwig, Carol. "A Brief History of Spiritual Directors International, Part 1." *Presence.* 8.1 (February 2002).

Ludwig, Carol. "A Brief History of Spiritual Directors International, Part 2." *Presence.* 8.2 (June 2002).

THEOLOGIES USEFUL FOR SPIRITUAL DIRECTION

Boff, Leonardo. *The Cry of the Earth, Cry of the Poor.* Maryknoll, NY: Orbis Books, 1995.

Cheng, Patrick. *Rainbow Theology: Bridging Race, Sexuality and Spirit.* New York: Seabury Books, 2013.

Christ, Carol. *Rebirth of the Goddess: Finding Meaning in Feminist Spirituality.* London: Routledge, 1998.

Cole, Graham A. *The God Who Became Human: A Biblical Theology of Incarnation.* Westmont, IL: IVP Academic, 2013.

Cornwall, Susannah. *Controversies in Queer Theology.* London: SCM Press, 2013.

Daly, Mary. *Beyond God the Father.* Boston: Beacon Press, 1993.

Fiorenza, Elizabeth Shussler. *Wisdom Ways: Introducing Feminist Biblical Interpretation.* Maryknoll, NY: Orbis Books, 2001.

Gutierrez, Gustavo. *A Theology of Liberation.* Maryknoll, NY: Orbis Books, 1973.

Johnson, Ben Campbell. *GodSpeech: Putting Divine Disclosures into Human Words.* Grand Rapids, MI: Eerdmans Publishing, 2006.

Migliore, Daniel L. *Faith Seeking Understanding: An Introduction to Christian Theology.* Grand Rapids, MI: Eerdmans Publishing, 1991.

McNeill, John J. *The Church and the Homosexual.* Boston: Beacon Press, 1976.

Moltmann, Jurgen. *The Living God and the Fullness of Life.* Louisville, KY: Westminster John Knox Press, 2015.

Plaskow, Judith. *Standing Again at Sinai: Judaism from a Feminist Perspective.* San Francisco: HarperOne, 1991.

Ruether, Rosemary Radford. *New Woman, New Earth.* Maryknoll, NY: Orbis Books, 1995.

Ruether, Rosemary Radford. *Sexism and God Talk: Toward a Feminist Theology.* Boston: Beacon Press, 1993.

Segundo, Juan Luis. *The Liberation of Theology.* Maryknoll, NY: Orbis Books, 1976.

Starhawk, Miriam. *The Spiral Dance: A Rebirth of the Ancient Religion of the Goddess (20th Anniversary Edition)*. San Francisco: HarperOne, 1997.

Stone, Howard W. *How to Think Theologically*. Minneapolis: Fortress Press, 2013

Sobrino, Jon. *The Spirituality of Liberation*. Maryknoll, NY: Orbis Books, 1988.

Torrance, Thomas. *Incarnation: The Person and Life of Christ*. Westmont, IL: IVP Academic, 2015.

SPIRITUAL DIRECTION IN THE EVOCATIVE METHOD

Awareness & Contemplation

Bill, Brent J. *Holy Silence: The Gift of Quaker Spirituality*. Brewster, MA: Paraclete Press, 2005.

Brother Lawrence. *The Practice of the Presence of God with Spiritual Maxims*. Grand Rapids, MI: Spire Books, 1958.

Cannato, Judy. *Radical Amazement: Contemplative Lessons from Black Holes, Supernovas, and other Wonders of the Universe*. Notre Dame: Sorin Books, 2006.

Foster, Richard and Gayle Beebe. *Longing for God: Seven Paths of Christian Devotion*. Downers Grove, IL: IV Press, 2009.

Katie, Byron. *Loving What Is: Four Questions That Can Change Your Life*. New York: Three Rivers Press, 2003.

Keating, Thomas. *Invitation to Love: The Way of Christian Contemplation*. New York: Continuum Publishing, 1998.

Levey, Joel and Michelle. *The Fine Arts of Relaxation, Concentration and Meditation: Ancient Skills for Modern Minds*. Boston: Wisdom Publications, 2003.

May, Gerald. *The Awakened Heart: Opening Yourself to the Love You Need*. San Francisco: Harper, 1991.

Nouwen, Henri J.M. *The Way of the Heart.* New York: Ballantine Books, 1981.

Rohr, Richard. *The Naked Now: Learning to See as the Mystics See.* New York: Crossroad Publishing, 2009.

Ruiz, Don Miguel. *The Four Agreements: A Guide to Personal Freedom, A Toltec Wisdom Book.* San Rafael, CA: Amber-Allen Publishing, 1997.

Tolle, Eckhart. *The Power of Now: A Guide to Spiritual Enlightenment.* Vancouver, BC: Namaste Publishing, 2004.

Reflection

Linn, Dennis, Sheila Fabricant Linn and Matthew Linn. *Sleeping with Bread: Holding What Gives You Life.* New York: Paulist Press, 1995.

Palmer, Parker. *A Hidden Wholeness: The Journey Toward an Undivided Life.* San Francisco: Jossey-Bass, 2004.

—. *Let Your Life Speak: Listening for the Voice of Vocation.* San Francisco: Jossey-Bass, 2000.

Discernment

Au, Wilkie and Noreen Cannon Au. *The Discerning Heart: Exploring the Christian Path.* New York: Paulist Press, 2006.

Barry, William A. *Paying Attention to God: Discernment in Prayer.* Notre Dame: Ave Maria, 1990.

Bill, J. Brent. *Sacred Compass: The Way of Spiritual Discernment.* Brewster, MA: Paraclete Press, 2008.

Campbell, Peter A. and Edwin M. McMahon. *Bio-Spirituality: Focusing as a Way to Grow.* Chicago: Loyola Press, 1977.

Conroy, Maureen. *The Discerning Heart: Discovering a Personal God.* Chicago: Loyola Press, 1993.

Dyckman, Katherine, Mary Garvin and Elizabeth Liebert. *The*

Spiritual Exercises Reclaimed: Uncovering Liberating Possibilities for Women. New York: Paulist Press, 2001.

Farrington, Debra K. *Hearing with the Heart: A Gentle Guide to Discerning God's Will for Your Life.* San Francisco: Jossey-Bass, 2003.

Green, Thomas H. *Weeds Among the Wheat: Discernment: Where Prayer and Action Meet.* Notre Dame: Ave Maria Press, 1984.

Isenhower, Valerie and Judith A. Todd. *Living into the Answers: A Workbook for Personal Spiritual Discernment.* Nashville: Upper Room, 2008.

Jones, Kirk Byron. *Holy Play: The Joyful Adventure of Unleashing Your Divine Purpose.* San Francisco: Jossey-Bass, 2007.

Kelsey, Morton. *Discernment: A Study in Ecstasy and Evil.* New York: Paulist Press, 1971.

Liebert, Elizabeth. *The Way of Discernment: Spiritual Practices for Decision Making.* Louisville: Westminster John Knox Press, 2008.

Lonsdale, David. *Listening to the Music of the Spirit: The Art of Discernment.* Notre Dame: Ave Maria Press, 1992.

Mueller, Joan. *Faithful Listening: Discernment in Everyday Life.* Kansas City, MO: Sheed & Ward, 1996.

Sheldrake, Philip. Befriending Our Desires. Notre Dame: Ave Maria Press, 1994.

Schmidt, Frederick W. *What God Wants for your Life: Changing the Way We Seek God's Will.* San Francisco: Harper, 2005.

Wolff, Pierre. *Discernment: The Art of Choosing Well.* Liguori, MO: Triumph, 1993.

PRACTICAL TOOLS FOR RESPONDING IN SPIRITUAL DIRECTION

Barry, William A. and William J. Connolly. *The Practice of Spiritual Direction.* San Francisco: Harper Collins, 1986.

Bidwell, Duane R. *Short-Term Spiritual Guidance.* Minneapolis: Fortress Press, 2004.

Hirsh, Sandra Krebs and Jane A.G. Kise. *Soul Types: Matching Your Personality and Spiritual Path.* Minneapolis: Augsburg Books, 2006.

Rosenberg, Marshall. *Living Nonviolent Communication: Practical Tools to Connect and Communicate Skillfully in Every Situation.* Louisville, CO: Sounds True, 2012.

Rosenberg, Marshall and Deepak Chopra. *Nonviolent Communication: A Language of Life, 3rd Edition.* Encinitas, CA: Puddledancer Press, 2015.

Taylor, Charles W. *The Skilled Pastor: Counseling as the Practice of Theology.* Minneapolis: Fortress Press, 1991.

SPIRITUAL DIRECTION FORMS

Individual Spiritual Direction—See Spiritual Direction (General)

Group Spiritual Direction

Dougherty, Rose Mary, SSND. *Group Spiritual Direction: Community for Discernment.* New York: Paulist Press, 1995.

Fryling, Alice. *Seeking God Together: An Introduction to Group Spiritual Direction.* Downers Grove, IL: IV Press, 2009.

Maxon, Monica and Rose Mary Dougherty, eds. *The Lived Experience of Group Spiritual Direction.* New York: Paulist Press, 2003.

Prechtel, Daniel. *Where Two or Three Are Gathered: Spiritual Direction for Small Groups.* New York: Morehouse Publishing, 2012.

Schrock, Daniel and Marlene Kropf, eds. *An Open Place: The Ministry of Group Spiritual Direction.* New York: Morehouse Publishing, 2012.

Vennard, Jane E. *A Praying Congregation: The Art of Teaching Spiritual Practice.* Herndon, VA: Alban Institute, 2005.

Organizational Spiritual Direction

Farnham, Suzanne G. and Stephanie A. Hull, et al. *Grounded in God: Listening Hearts Discernment for Group Deliberations.* Harrisburg, PA: Morehouse, 1999.

—. *Listening Hearts: Discerning Call in Community.* Harrisburg, PA: Morehouse, 1991.

Fendall, Lon, Jan Wood and Bruce Bishop. *Practicing Discernment Together: Finding God's Way Forward in Decision Making.* Newberg, OR: Barclay Press, 2007.

McKinney, Mary Benet. *Sharing Wisdom: A Process for Group Decision Making.* Allen, TX: Thomas More, 1987.

Morris, Danny and Charles Olsen. *Discerning God's Will Together: A Spiritual Practice for the Church.* Nashville: Upper Room Books, 1997.

WORKING OUTSIDE YOUR TRADITION, CULTURE AND COMFORT ZONE

Varieties of Faith and Cultural Backgrounds

Boorstein, Sylvia. *That's Funny, You Don't Look Buddhist: On Being a Faithful Jew and Passionate Buddhist.* San Francisco: HarperOne, 1998.

Bowker, John. *Oxford Concise Dictionary of World Religions.* Oxford: Oxford University Press, 2000.

Epperly, Bruce G. and Lewis D. Solomon. *Mending the World: Spiritual Hope for Ourselves and Our Planet.* Philadelphia: Inisfree Press, 2004.

Fuller, Robert C. *Spiritual, but not Religious.* Oxford: Oxford University Press, 2001.

Griffiths, Bede. *A New Vision of Reality.* Springfield, IL: Templegate Publishers, 1998.

Howe, Mary Blye. *Sitting with Sufis: A Christian Experience of Learning Sufism.* Brewster, MA: Paraclete Press, 2005.

Hughes, Amanda, ed. *Five Voices, Five Faiths: An Interfaith Primer.* Cambridge, MA: Cowley, 2005.

Knitter, Paul. *Introducing Theologies of Religions.* Maryknoll: Orbis Books, 2002.

Liepert, David. *Muslim, Christian and Jew: Finding a Path to Peace Our Faiths Can Share.* Toronto: Faith of Life Publishing, 2010.

Mabry, John. *A Christian Walks in the Footsteps of the Buddha.* Berkeley: Apocryphile Press, 2014.

—. *Faith Styles: Ways People Believe.* New York: Morehouse Publishing, 2006.

—. *Spiritual Guidance Across Religions: A Sourcebook for Spiritual Directors and Other Professionals Providing Counsel to People of Differing Faith Traditions, First Edition.* Nashville: Skylight Paths, 2014.

Matlins, Stuart and Arthur Magida, eds. *How to Be a Perfect Stranger: The Essential Religious Etiquette Handbook.* Nashville: SkyLight Paths Publishing, 2006.

Mercadente, Linda A. *Belief without Borders: Inside the Minds of the Spiritual but not Religious.* New York: Oxford Press, 2014.

O'Gara, Margaret. *The Ecumenical Gift Exchange.* Collegeville, MN: Liturgical Press, 1998.

O'Donnell, Kevin. *Inside World Religions: An Illustrated Guide.* Minneapolis: Fortress Press, 2007.

Ochs, Carol and Kerry M. Ilitzky. *Jewish Spiritual Guidance: Finding Our Way to God.* San Francisco: Jossey-Bass, 1997.

Parachin, Victor. *Eastern Wisdom for Western Minds.* Maryknoll: Orbis Books, 2007.

Partridge, Christopher, ed. *Introduction to World Religions.* Minneapolis: Fortress Press, 2005.

Rahman, Jamal, Kathleen Schmitt Elias and Ann Holmes Redding. *Out of Darkness, Into Light: Spiritual Guidance in the Quran with Reflections from Jewish and Christian Sources.* New York: More-house Publishing, 2009.

Smith, Huston. *The World's Religions: Our Great Wisdom Traditions.* San Francisco: Harper, 1991.

Teasdale, Wayne. *The Mystic Heart: Discovering a Universal Spirituality in the World's Religions.* Novato, CA: New World Library, 2001.

Vest, Norvene, ed. *Still Listening: New Horizons in Spiritual Direction.* New York: Morehouse Publishing, 2000.

—. *Tending the Holy: Spiritual Direction Across Traditions.* New York: Morehouse Publishing, 2003.

Wagner, Nick. *Spiritual Direction in Context.* New York: Morehouse Publishing, 2006.

Walsh, Roger. *Essential Spirituality: The 7 Central Practices to Awaken Heart and Mind.* Hoboken, NJ: Wiley Press, 2000.

Gender—General

Adam, David and Monia Capoferri. *The Road of Life: Reflections on Searching and Longing.* New York: Morehouse Publishing, 2004.

Ellison, Marvin and Kelly Brown Douglas, eds. *Sexuality and the Sacred, Second Edition: Sources for Theological Reflection.* Louis-ville, Westminster John Knox Press, 2010.

Fox, Matthew. *Original Blessing: A Primer in Creation Spirituality.* Santa Fe: Bear & Co, 1983.

Nelson, James and Sandra Longfellow, eds. *Sexuality and the Sacred, First Edition: Sources for Theological Reflection.* Louisville: Westminster John Knox Press, 1994.

Tallman, Bruce. *Archetypes for Spiritual Direction: Discovering Heroes Within.* New York: Paulist Press, 2005.

Gender—Divine Feminine

Eisler, Riane. *The Chalice and the Blade: Our History, Our Future.* San Francisco: HarperOne, 1998.

Fischer, Kathleen. "Spiritual Direction with Women." *Handbook of Spirituality for Ministers (Volume 1).* Ed. Robert J. Wicks. New York: Paulist Press, 1995. 96-114.

Kidd, Sue Monk. *Dance of the Dissident Daughter: A Woman's Journey from Christian Tradition to the Sacred Feminine.* San Francisco: HarperOne, 1996.

Lanzetta, Beverly. *Radical Wisdom.* Minneapolis: Fortress Press, 2005.

Murdock, Maureen. *The Heroine's Journey.* Boulder, CO: Shambhala, 1990.

Zweig, Connie. *To Be a Woman: The Birth of the Conscious Feminine.* New York: Tarcher, 1990.

Gender—Divine Masculine

Fox, Matthew. *The Hidden Spirituality of Men: Ten Metaphors to Awaken the Sacred Masculine.* Novato, CA: New World Library, 2008.

Moore, Robert and Douglas Gillette. *King, Warrior, Magician, Lover: Rediscovering the Archetypes of the Mature Masculine.* San Francisco: HarperOne, 1991.

Rohr, Richard and Joseph Martos. *From Wild Man to Wise Man: Reflections on Male Spirituality.* Cincinnati: St. Anthony Messenger Press, 2005

Gender and Sexual Minorities

Cheng, Patrick. *Radical Love: Introduction to Queer Theology.* New York: Seabury Books, 2011.

—. *Rainbow Theology: Bridging Race, Sexuality and Spirit.* New York: Seabury Books, 2013.

Kundtz, David J. and Bernard S. Schlager. *Ministry Among God's Queer Folk: LGBT Pastoral Care.* Cleveland: Pilgrim Press, 2007.

Lightsey, Pamela. *Our Lives Matter: A Womanist Queer Theology.* Eugene, OR: Pickwick Publications, 2015.

Vest, Norvene, ed. *Still Listening: New Horizons in Spiritual Direction.* New York: Morehouse Publishing, 2000.

Youth and Young Adults

Dean, Kendra Creasy and Ron Foster. *The Godbearing Life: The Art of Soul Tending for Youth Ministry.* Nashville: Upper Room Books, 1998.

Hendricks, Patricia. *Hungry Souls, Holy Companions: Mentoring a New Generation of Christians.* New York: Morehouse, 2006.

Miller, Donald. *Blue Like Jazz: Nonreligious Thoughts on Christian Spirituality.* Nashville: Thomas Nelson, 2003.

Yaconelli, Mark. *Contemplative Youth Ministry: Practicing the Presence of Jesus.* Grand Rapids: Zondervan, 2006.

Aging Populations

Rohr, Richard. *Falling Upward: A Spirituality for the Two Halves of Life.* San Francisco: Jossey-Bass, 2011.

Chittister, Joan. *The Gift of Years: Growing Older Gracefully.* Stillwater, OK: BlueBridge Publishers, 2010.

Persons in Recovery

Nelson, James. *Thirst: God and the Alcoholic Experience.* Louisville: Westminster John Knox Press, 2004.

Rohr, Richard. *Breathing Underwater: Spirituality and the Twelve Steps.* Cincinnati: Franciscan Media, 2011.

Persons with Disabilities

Carter, Erik W. *Including People with Disabilities in Faith Communities*. Baltimore: Brooks Publishing, 2007.

Reynolds, Thomas E. *Vulnerable Communion: A Theology of Disability and Hospitality*. Grand Rapids: Brazos Press, 2008.

Clergy, Seminarians, and Persons-in-Discernment

Cetuk, Virginia Samuel. *What to Expect in Seminary: Theological Education as Spiritual Formation*. Nashville: Abingdon Press, 1998.

Farnham, Suzanne G. and Joseph P. Gill, R. Taylor McLean and Susan Ward. *Listening Hearts: Discerning Call in Community*. New York: Morehouse Publishing, 1991.

Lehr, Fred. *Clergy Burnout: Recovering from the 70 Hour Week... and other Self-Defeating Practices*. Minneapolis: Augsburg Books, 2005.

Mellott, David M. *Finding Your Way in Seminary: What to Expect, How to Thrive*. Louisville: Westminster John Knox Press, 2016.

Nouwen, Henri. *The Wounded Healer: Ministry in Contemporary Society*. New York: Image Books, 1979.

Oswald, Roy. *Clergy Self-Care: Finding a Balance for Effective Ministry*. Lanham, MD: Rowman & Littlefield Publishers, 1995.

Rediger, G. Lloyd. *Clergy Killers: Guidance for Pastors and Congregations Under Attack*. Louisville: Westminster John Knox Press, 1997.

Ruth, Kibbie and Karen McClintock. *Healthy Disclosure: Solving Communication Quandaries in Congregations*. Lanham, MD: Rowman & Littlefield Publishers, 2007.

SPIRITUAL DIRECTION AND OTHER HELPING PROFESSIONS

Bidwell, Duane R. *Short-Term Spiritual Guidance*. Minneapolis: Fortress Press, 2004.

189

May, Gerald W. *Care of Mind/Care of Spirit: A Psychiatrist Explores Spiritual Direction.* New York: Harper Collins, 1982.

May, Rollo. *Addiction and Grace: Love and Spirituality in the Healing of Addictions.* San Francisco: HarperOne, 2007.

Myss, Caroline. *Anatomy of the Spirit: The Seven Stages of Power and Healing.* New York: Three Rivers Press, 1996.

Peterson, Eugene H. *The Contemplative Pastor: Returning to the Art of Spiritual Direction.* Grand Rapids: Eerdmans, 1989.

Sherwood, Keith. *The Art of Spiritual Healing.* Woodbury, MN: Llewellyn Publications, 1985.

Taylor, Charles W. *The Skilled Pastor: Counseling as the Practice of Theology.* Minneapolis: Fortress Press, 1991.

Underwood, Lynn. *Spiritual Connection in Daily Life.* West Conshohocken, PA: Templeton Press, 2013.

ETHICAL CONSIDERATIONS IN SPIRITUAL DIRECTION

Beattie, Melody. *Codependent No More: How to Stop Controlling Others and Start Caring for Yourself.* Center City, MN: Hazelden, 1987.

Fortune, Marie. *Is Nothing Sacred?* San Francisco: Harper, 1989.

Hedberg, Thomas M. and Betsy Caprio and the staff of The Center for Sacred Psychology. *A Code of Ethics for Spiritual Directors.* Pecos, NM: Dove Publications, 1992.

Katherine, Anne. *Boundaries: Where You End and I Begin.* New York: Simon & Schuster, 1991.

Lebacqz, Karen and Joseph Driskill. *Ethics and Spiritual Care.* Nashville: Abingdon Press, 2000.

Ruth, Kibbie Simmons and Karen A. McClintock. *Healthy Disclosure: Solving Communication Quandaries in Congregations.* Herndon, VA: Alban Institute, 2007.

Black, Jan and Greg Enns. *Better Boundaries: Owning and Treasuring Your Life.* Oakland: New Harbinger, 1997.

Spiritual Directors International. "Guidelines for Ethical

Conduct." SDIworld.org, 2014: https://tinyurl.com/SDI-guidelines.

Taylor, Kylea. *The Ethics of Caring.* Santa Cruz, CA: Hanford Mead Publishers, 1995.

FORMATION, TRAINING, AND SUPERVISION OF SPIRITUAL DIRECTORS

Buckley, Suzanne, ed. *Sacred is the Call: Formation and Transformation in Spiritual Direction Programs.* New York: Crossroad Publishing, 2005.

Bumpus, Mary Rose and Rebecca Bradburn Langer. *Supervision of Spiritual Directors: Engaging in Holy Mystery.* New York: Morehouse Publishing, 2005.

Conroy, Maureen, R.S.M. *Looking into the Well: Supervision of Spiritual Directors.* Chicago: Loyola Press, 1995.

Gubi, Peter Madsen, ed. *What Counsellors and Spiritual Directors Can Learn from Each Other.* London: Jessica Kingsley Publishers, 2017.

SETTING UP A SPIRITUAL DIRECTION PRACTICE

Tallman, Bruce. *Finding Seekers: How to Develop a Spiritual Direction Practice from Beginning to Full-Time Employment.* Berkeley: Apocryphile Press, 2011.

MARKETING YOUR SPIRITUAL DIRECTION PRACTICE

Burg, Bob. *Endless Referrals: Network Your Everyday Contacts into Sales.* New York: McGraw-Hill, 2006.

Tallman, Bruce. *Finding Seekers: How to Develop a Spiritual Direction Practice from Beginning to Full-Time Employment.* Berkeley: Apocryphile Press, 2011.

ADDITIONAL RESOURCES FOR SPIRITUAL PRACTICE AND SPIRITUAL FORMATION

Barton, Ruth Haley. *Sacred Rhythms: Arranging Our Lives for Spiritual Transformation.* Downers Grove, IL: IV Press, 2006.

Benner, David G. *Spirituality and the Awakening Self: The Sacred Journey of Transformation.* Grand Rapids: Brazos Press, 2012

Bill, J. Brent. *Mind the Light: Learning to See with Spiritual Eyes.* Brewster, MA: Paraclete Press, 2006.

Bloom, Anthony. *Beginning to Pray.* New York: Paulist Press, 1970.

Blythe, Teresa. *50 Ways to Pray: Practices from Many Traditions and Times.* Nashville: Abingdon Press, 2006.

Brach, Tara. *Radical Acceptance: Embracing Your Life with the Heart of a Buddha.* New York: Bantam Dell, 2003.

Brown, Patricia. *Paths to Prayer: Finding Your Own Way to the Presence of God.* San Francisco: Jossey-Bass, 2003.

Brussat, Frederic and Mary Ann. *Spiritual Literacy: Reading the Sacred in Everyday Life.* New York: Touchstone Books, 1996.

Bourgeault, Cynthia. *The Heart of Centering Prayer: Nondual Christianity in Theory and Practice.* Boulder, CO: Shambhala Press, 2016.

Calhoun, Adele Ahlberg. *Spiritual Disciplines Handbook: Practices that Transform Us.* Downers Grove, IL: IV Press, 2005.

Corcoran, Nancy. *Secrets of Prayer: A Multifaith Guide to Creating Personal Prayer in Your Life.* Woodstock, VT: SkyLight Paths Publishing, 2007.

De Waal, Esther. *Seeking God: The Way of St. Benedict.* London: Faith Press, 1984.

Ford, Marcia. *Finding Hope: Cultivating God's Gift of a Hopeful Spirit.* Woodstock, VT: SkyLight Paths Publishing, 2007.

Foster, Richard J. *Celebration of Discipline: The Path to Spiritual Growth (3rd edition).* San Francisco: Harper, 1998.

Foster, Richard J. and Gayle D. Beebe. *Longing for God: Seven Paths of Christian Devotion.* Downers Grove, IL: IV Press, 2009.

Holt, Bradley P. *Thirsty for God: A Brief History of Christian Spirituality.* Minneapolis: Augsburg Fortress, 1993.

Levey, Joel and Michelle. *The Fine Arts of Relaxation, Concentration and Meditation: Ancient Skills for Modern Minds.* Boston: Wisdom Publications, 2003.

Miller, William. *Your Golden Shadow: Discovering and Fulfilling Your Underdeveloped Self.* San Francisco: Harper and Row, 1989.

McQuiston, John. *Finding Time for the Timeless: Spirituality in the Workweek.* Woodstock, VT: SkyLight Paths Publishing, 2004.

Mulholland, M. Robert. *Invitation to a Journey: A Road Map for Spiritual Formation.* Downers Grove, IL: IV Press, 2016.

Myss, Caroline. *Sacred Contracts: Awakening Your Divine Potential.* Easton, PA: Harmony, 2003.

Nouwen, Henri. *Spiritual Formation: Following the Movements of the Spirit.* New York: HarperOne, 2015.

Paulsell, William O. *Rules for Prayer.* New York: Paulist Press, 1993.

Rohr, Richard. *Everything Belongs: The Gift of Contemplative Prayer.* New York: Crossroad Publishing, 2003.

Salwak, Dale, ed. *The Wonders of Solitude.* Novato, CA: New World Library, 1998.

Stroud, J. Francis, S.J. *Praying Naked: The Spirituality of Anthony de Mello.* New York: Doubleday, 2005.

Thompson, Marjorie J. *Soul Feast: An Invitation to the Christian Spiritual Life.* Louisville: Westminster John Knox Press, 1995.

Whitmire, Catherine. *Plain Living: A Quaker Path to Simplicity.* Notre Dame, IN: Sorin Books, 2001.

Wolpert, Daniel. *Creating a Life with God: The Call of Ancient Prayer Practices.* Nashville: Upper Room Books, 2003.

ACKNOWLEDGMENTS

The inspiration for this book comes from the hundreds of people I have met over the years as I gave and received the gift of spiritual direction. I am indebted to the faculty and participants of the Diploma in the Art of Spiritual Direction (DASD) program at San Francisco Theological Seminary where I received my training. That program provided a rich foundation for all the work I have been privileged to do over the past 20 years.

I am continuously inspired by my friends and co-workers at the Hesychia School of Spiritual Direction at the Redemptorist Renewal Center in Tucson. This book is filled with the wisdom gathered from the faculty and participants of this program. I am especially grateful for the leadership and support from Fr. Gregory Wiest, Rev. Greg Foraker and Shawna Hansen—my beloved team of administrators at Hesychia.

The people I have had the honor of working with in spiritual direction are perhaps my greatest teachers. Thank you for allowing me to learn so much while doing this work.

I appreciate the support and wisdom of the supervisors I've worked with over the years. Rev. Elizabeth Nordquist and Maria Tattu Bowen—you are rock stars of the supervision world!

And words cannot convey how much past and present spiritual directors of mine have enhanced my life. You are the reason I am able to love and serve God. Thank you, Victoria Curtiss, Dina Gardner, Elizabeth Nordquist, David Buechner, Sr. Diane Bridenbecker and Gil Stafford.

My husband, Duane Schneider, has always given me the love and support I need to make spiritual direction, writing and related pursuits my full-time job. Thank you for making this book possible.

And finally, Rev. John Mabry, senior editor at Apocryphile Press, I am grateful that you so quickly and enthusiastically accepted this manuscript for publication. Hopefully your Chaplaincy Institute's Interfaith Spiritual Direction Certificate Program will find it useful!

—*Teresa Blythe*

ABOUT THE AUTHOR

REV. TERESA BLYTHE is an accomplished spiritual director, author, and public speaker on topics of practical spirituality. She has been working with individuals, groups and organizations in spiritual direction since 1997 and has served for over 10 years as Director of the Hesychia School of Spiritual Direction at the Redemptorist Renewal Center at Picture Rocks in Tucson, AZ. She is the founder of the Phoenix Center for Spiritual Direction in downtown Phoenix.

An ordained minister in the United Church of Christ (UCC), Teresa received her Master of Divinity and Diploma in the Art of Spiritual Direction from San Francisco Theological Seminary in 2000. In 2006 she authored *50 Ways to Pray: Practices from Many Traditions and Times* for Abingdon Press.

Teresa and her husband Duane Schneider, a physical therapist, live in Phoenix. They are members of First United Church of Christ Phoenix where Teresa is on staff as an assistant pastor.

Contact the author at:
teresa@teresablythe.net

You might also enjoy...

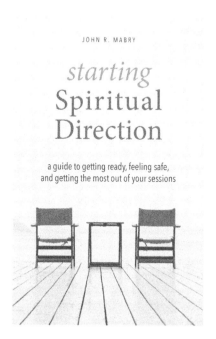

JOHN R. MABRY

starting
Spiritual
Direction

a guide to getting ready, feeling safe,
and getting the most out of your sessions

Starting spiritual direction for the first time?
This book tells you everything you need to know.

Starting Spiritual Direction is one of the first books on spiritual direction written for people who are receiving spiritual direction, rather than giving it. In a friendly, easy-to-read style, Dr. Mabry tells you everything you need to know to make your spiritual direction sessions a sacred and fruitful time.

Get *Starting Spiritual Direction* today!
Just click on https://books2read.com/startingSD

Made in the USA
Coppell, TX
20 September 2020

38400495R00125